ISBN 0-913916-25-0
Library of Congress Catalog Card Number 76-29532

Printed in Nashville, Tennessee
by Incentive Publications
Box 12522
Nashville, Tennessee 37212

TABLE OF CONTENTS

COMMUNICATIONS SKILLS MINI-CENTERS

ENVIRONMENTAL STUDIES MINI-CENTERS

QUANTITATIVE STUDIES MINI-CENTERS

MULTI-DISCIPLINARY MINI-CENTERS

APPENDIX

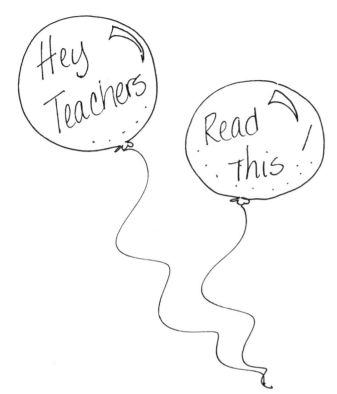

PREFACE

Teachers moving to the learning center approach to individualizing instruction often find that one of their most immediate needs is for "back up" activities to supplement and reinforce the sequentially organized learning centers. It is in response to this need that Mini-Center Stuff has been developed.

Simply defined, a mini-center is a collection of materials and directions packaged in a self-contained manner to enable an individual student to work his way through the center at his own rate and in keeping with his ability and learning style. The complete mini-center includes all the materials necessary for completion of the center activities. For example, if a dictionary or art materials are required they will be placed in the center container rather than directions for the student to go to the library or the art center. Due to the flexibility afforded both student and teacher, this approach provides optimum opportunity for personalized learning. The easily portable mini-center can be used at a classroom desk on either an assigned or free choice basis; taken to the library or school yard; assigned as homework; or enjoyed on a free choice basis as a special reward for work well done.

A good balance of sequentially organized learning centers designed to teach specific skills and concepts, easily accessible free choice interest centers, and attractively presented mini-centers should provide a stimulating and encouraging classroom environment. Within this framework directed teaching sessions, independent and group study projects, and free reading periods flourish and gain meaningful support and reinforcement.

The importance of attractiveness in packaging, clarity in directions, careful selection of materials, and realistic instructional goals cannot be overemphasized. Remembering that the goal of mini-center construction is to make each center irresistible to the learner, the authors of Mini-Center Stuff have suggested many different games, activities, and gimmicks, and have employed a wide variety of materials.

The collection includes twenty communications skills mini-centers, sixteen environmental studies mini-centers, fifteen quantitative studies mini-centers, and eighteen multi-disciplinary mini-centers. Each of the academic area mini-centers includes three or more separate activities related to the central skill or concept. The multi-disciplinary mini-centers are composed of one math activity, one language activity, one environmental activity, and one creative arts activity. A "just for fun" idea accompanies each of the mini-centers. The activities have been left as open-ended as possible to allow for flexibility in use and adaptation to other learning situations. In most instances they may be included in or used to supplement projects in other academic areas and/or adjusted to meet differing needs of more or less mature learners. Individual teachers are invited to select Mini-Center Stuff as presented, or to mix, match, or rearrange individual center activities to better meet their own students' needs and interests.

Have fun!

Imogene Forte
Mary Ann Pangle

Alphabet Acrobats

Cut several sizes of letters of the alphabet from black construction paper and paste randomly on a white shirt or sweater box. Place the following items in the box:

drawing paper
crayons
tagboard letter
    cards for each
    letter of the
    alphabet (laminated
    if possible) placed in
    a plastic sandwich
    bag
pencil
dictionary
kitchen timer
task instructions

Print these directions inside the cover of the box:

Follow the directions and complete the tasks.
Evaluate completed activities with the teacher.

Print these directions on an index card and paper clip to two sheets of drawing paper:

Arrange the letter cards in alphabetical order. Rule two sheets of drawing paper into twenty-six squares and make a mini-picture dictionary showing one word for each letter. Picture the most unusual words you can think of to make your dictionary interesting.

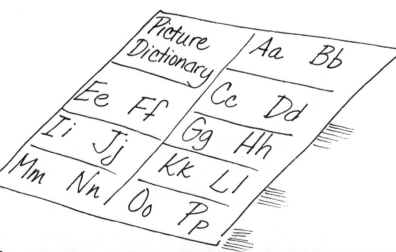

Print these directions on a sheet of drawing paper:

Take all the letter cards out of the plastic bag. Place them face down on the table. Set the timer for fifteen minutes. Turn the cards face up, one at a time, and play the game according to the following rules.

Give yourself one free point for the first letter. Turn up the second letter and write a two-letter word beginning with that letter. Write a three-letter word for the third letter and continue in this manner until your fifteen minutes is up. Give yourself one point for each letter.

Record your score and play the game again to see how much you can improve it.

Print these directions on a large index card and paper clip to another card of the same size:

Design your alphabet profile by printing your full name vertically on the attached card. Write one adjective describing you that begins with each letter.

Draw your portrait as revealed by this profile on the back of the card.

Clever
Animated
Risky
Outgoing
Lively
Happy
Arty
Rowdy
Talented

Just for Fun...
Turn each letter of the alphabet into an original animal character.

BANG-UP BLENDS

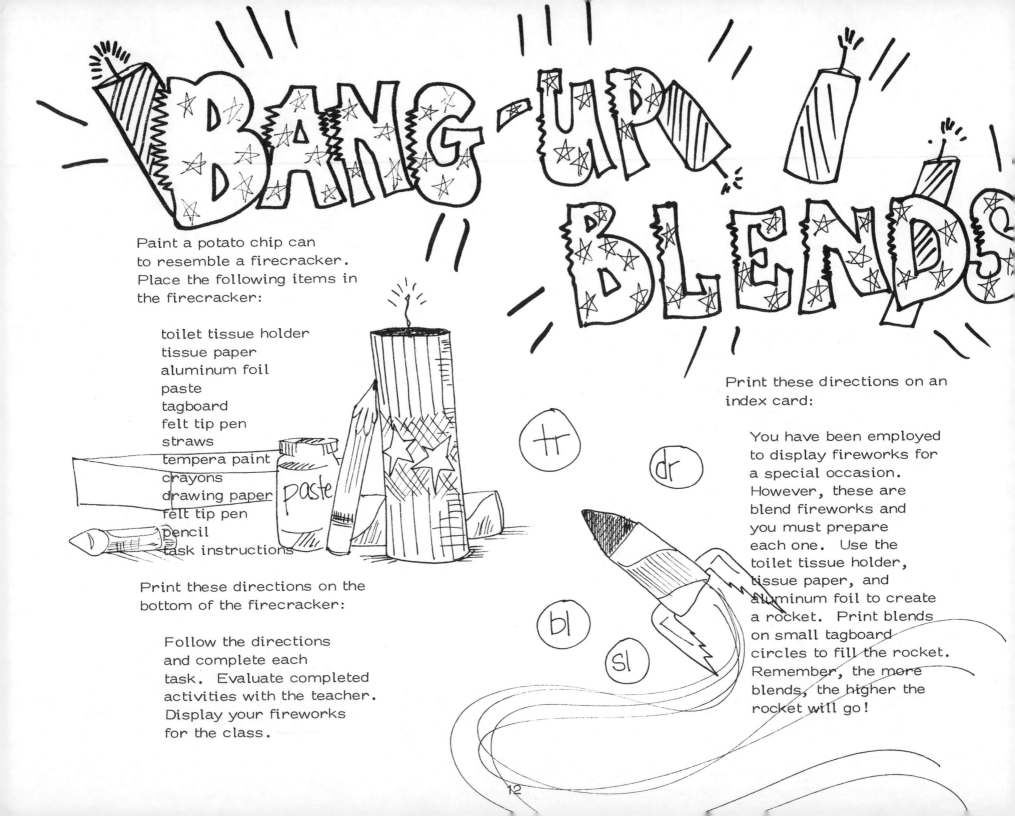

Paint a potato chip can to resemble a firecracker. Place the following items in the firecracker:

toilet tissue holder
tissue paper
aluminum foil
paste
tagboard
felt tip pen
straws
tempera paint
crayons
drawing paper
felt tip pen
pencil
task instructions

Print these directions on the bottom of the firecracker:

Follow the directions and complete each task. Evaluate completed activities with the teacher. Display your fireworks for the class.

Print these directions on an index card:

You have been employed to display fireworks for a special occasion. However, these are blend fireworks and you must prepare each one. Use the toilet tissue holder, tissue paper, and aluminum foil to create a rocket. Print blends on small tagboard circles to fill the rocket. Remember, the more blends, the higher the rocket will go!

Print these directions on an index card:

The grand finale must be the best!
Use different colors of tempera
paint dipped in straws and blow the
paint on a piece of drawing paper.
When the paint has dried, write words
that contain blends on the fireworks.
Many words will be needed to cover
the sky with fireworks.

Print these directions on an index card:

Create a new type of fireworks.
As the color is displayed in the
sky, a loud noise is heard.
The noise is a metal box opening
and strips of paper float to the
ground. Sentences are written
on the strips of paper. Each
sentence contains a word that
begins with a blend. The crowd
goes wild because everyone wants
a strip of paper. Write enough
sentences so no one will be
disappointed!

Just for Fun...

Illustrate a fireworks display
that you have seen or would
like to see.

CONSONANT COUNTRY

Place the following items in a straw hat:

writing paper
drawing paper
pencil
crayons
task instructions

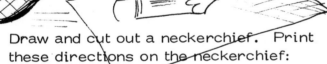

Draw and cut out a neckerchief. Print these directions on the neckerchief:

Follow the directions and complete each task. Evaluate completed activities with the teacher. Total your points and record them on the class roster.

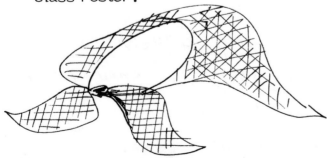

Cut twenty-one circles from tagboard. Print one consonant on each circle. Place the circles in a plastic bag. Print these directions on a colored piece of construction paper and place in the plastic bag:

Welcome to the country! Take a walk through the fields. Draw a consonant circle from the plastic bag. Write the name of a food grown in the country that begins with that consonant. You receive one point for each food that you name.

Cut a shape that resembles an animal.
Print these directions on the animal:

Draw an outline of a barn.
Fill the barn with animals
that might live in the country.
The names of the animals must
begin with a consonant. Color
the barn. You receive one
point for each animal named.

Draw and cut out a hoe. Print these directions
on the hoe:

There are many chores to perform
in the country. Make a list of the
different country chores. Each
chore must begin with a consonant.
You receive one point for each chore.

Just for Fun...
Make a list of living things
that are seen in the country
that end with a consonant.
You receive two points for each
item.

Contraction Casserole

Place the following items in a casserole dish.

writing paper	felt tip pen
drawing paper	tape
pencil	cassette tape player
large macaroni	yellow construction paper
yarn	task instructions

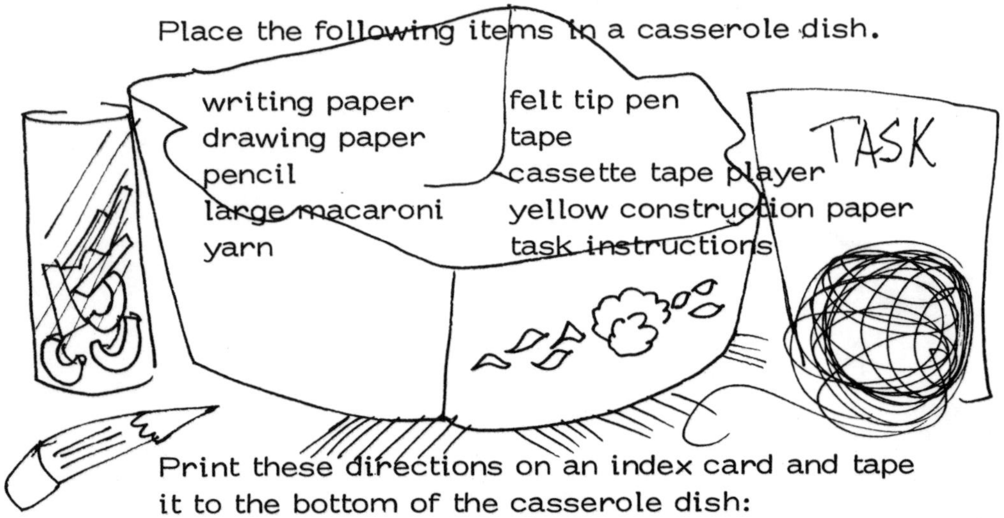

TASK

Print these directions on an index card and tape it to the bottom of the casserole dish:

Follow the directions and complete each task. Evaluate completed activities with the teacher.

Print words from which contractions can be made on strips of tagboard. Print these directions on an index card. Place the word cards, macaroni, yarn, and directions in a plastic bag:

Macaroni is the first ingredient in the casserole. Shuffle the cards and place them face down. Draw a card and read the two words. Use the felt tip pen and print the contraction for the two words on a piece of macaroni. Continue until all the word cards have been used. String the macaroni on yarn and wear the contraction necklace!

Draw and cut out twenty shapes to resemble fish. Print a contraction on ten fish. Print the two words from which the contraction is made on ten fish. Print these directions on an index card:

Fish is the second ingredient in the casserole. Place the fish face down in four rows of five fish. Look at two fish. If the two words and the contraction match, they are a book and you remove them from the game. If the two cards do not match, leave the fish in the game. Continue until all the cards have been matched.

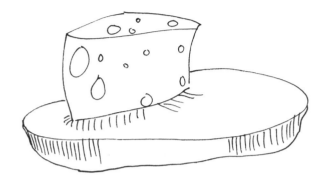

Tape a list of contractions. Print these directions on an index card:

Add contraction cheese to the casserole.
Draw and cut out a large piece of cheese from the yellow construction paper.
Listen to the tape and try to spell each contraction correctly. Write the contractions on the piece of cheese.

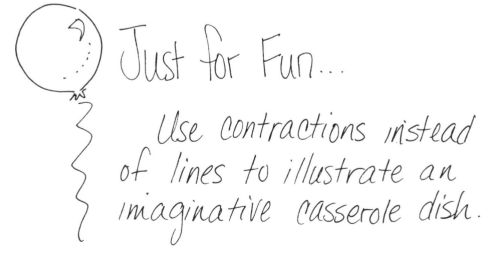

Just for Fun...

Use contractions instead of lines to illustrate an imaginative casserole dish.

Crumbled cookies

Place the following items in a cookie jar:

pencil
writing paper
cookie
task instructions

Draw and cut out a circle to resemble a cookie.

Print these directions on the cookie and paste them on the outside of the cookie jar:

Follow the directions and complete each task. Evaluate completed activities with the teacher.

Cut out circles to resemble a cookie from red poster board. Print a word that has an antonym on each cookie. Print these directions on one cookie and paste them on the outside of the cookie jar:

Write an antonym for each red cookie.

Cut out circles to resemble a cookie from blue poster board. Print a word that has a homonym on each cookie. Print these directions on one cookie and paste them on the outside of the cookie jar:

Write a homonym for each blue cookie.

Cut out circles to resemble a cookie from yellow poster board. Print a word that has a synonym on each cookie. Print these directions on one cookie and paste them on the outside of the cookie jar:

Write a synonym for each yellow cookie.

Enlarge the game on orange poster board. Print these directions on the back of the game:

See how quickly you can eat the cookie! Begin eating on the outside and stop each time you reach a letter. You must say a pair of homonyms if you stop on H, a pair of synonyms if you stop on S, and a pair of antonyms if you stop on A. When you have eaten the game cookie, enjoy the real cookie!

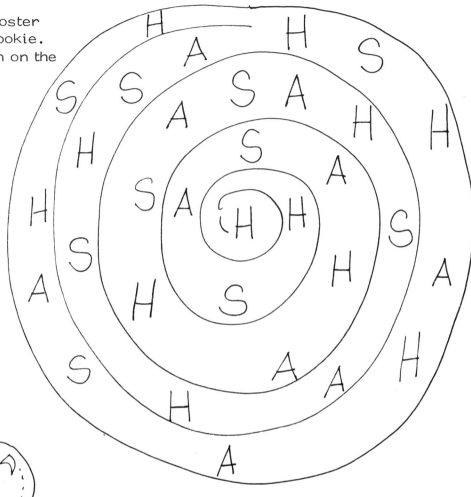

Just for fun....
Write a creative story about a magic cookie.

DISH DETAIL

Place the following items in a dish drainer:

pencil   crayons
piece of colored poster   task instructions
   board

Draw and cut out a glass from colored poster board. Print these directions on the glass:

Follow the directions and complete each task. Evaluate completed activities with the teacher.

Draw and cut out six dinner plates from colored poster board. Print six sentences on five of the dinner plates. Print these directions on the back of the sixth dinner plate:

Design a subject and predicate dinner plate! Write each sentence on the plate and underline the complete subject with a red crayon and the complete predicate with a black crayon. Create a design by using crayons and lightly coloring a picture on the dinner plate.

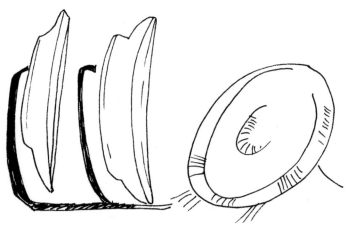

Draw and cut out five cups from colored poster board. Print five sentences on four of the cups. Print these directions on the back of the fifth cup:

Fill the cup with verbs! Read each sentence and write the verb in the cup.

Draw and cut out two bowls from colored poster board. Print thirty sentences in one of the bowls. Print these directions on the back of the other bowl:

Make a simple subject soufflé. Read each sentence and write the simple subject in the bowl.

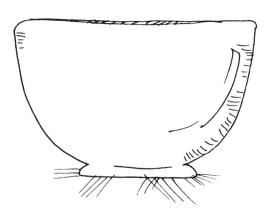

Draw and cut out ten knives, ten forks, and ten spoons from colored poster board. Print one complete subject on each knife. Print one complete predicate on each fork. Draw and cut out one large spoon and print these directions on it:

Set a subject and predicate table! Read each complete subject on the knives and match it with the correct complete predicate on the forks. Write each complete sentence on a spoon.

Just for Fun...

Draw and cut out one more item that could be found in a dish drainer. Write three sentences on it. Underline the subject and complete predicate.

21

Doctor's Diagnosis

Place the following items in a toy doctor or nurse kit:

> tape
> cassette tape recorder
> writing paper
> pencil
> task instructions

Tape twenty-five sentences that end with a period, question mark, or exclamation mark. Draw and cut out a stethoscope. Print these directions on the stethoscope:

> Use the stethoscope and record a different kind of beat. Number a piece of paper from 1 – 25. Turn the tape on and listen to each sentence. Write the correct punctuation mark after you hear each sentence.

Print these directions on an ice cream stick to resemble a tongue depressor:

> Follow the directions and complete each task. Evaluate completed activities with the teacher.

Enlarge the following game board on poster board. Print a sentence on each degree on the thermometer.

Cut out shapes from tagboard to resemble periods, question marks, commas, and exclamation marks. Place them in a pill bottle. Print these directions on the back of the game:

What is your name 98.6

It's temperature—taking time! Read each sentence and add a punctuation mark from the pill bottle. See how high the temperature will go!

Print twenty sentences without punctuation marks on a piece of tagboard. Staple twenty small pieces of white paper together to resemble a prescription pad. Print these directions on the pad:

These sentences are ill. They need a punctuation mark. Write a prescription for each sentence by writing the sentence and adding the correct punctuation mark.

Just for Fun...
Draw yourself as a doctor or a nurse and make a work schedule for the day. What will you do after hours for fun?

¡Get in Step!

Draw and cut out five shapes to resemble a foot. Print the task instructions on the foot.

Place the following items in a shoe:

pencil
crayons
scissors
writing
 paper
drawing paper
task instructions

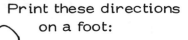

Print these directions on a foot.
Attach the foot with yarn to the shoestring of the shoe:

Follow the directions and complete each task.
Evaluate completed activities with the teacher.

Print these directions on a foot:

You have been asked to organize the school parade. All the students in your classroom have been selected to march in the parade. You must have a list of the students' names in alphabetical order before you line them up for the parade. Make an alphabetical listing of the students by writing their last names first.

Print these directions on a foot:

The band looks great in brand new uniforms. Draw and color a picture of each instrument that will be played in the band. Cut out the pictures and paste them in alphabetical order on a piece of drawing paper.

Print these directions on a foot:

Make a list of all the streets or roads in your neighborhood. Draw the parade route showing each street or road. The streets or roads must be listed in alphabetical order for the parade route.

Print these directions on a foot:

The parade will march through the main street or shopping center of your town. Make an alphabetical listing of the stores and businesses located on the main street or in the shopping center.

Just for Fun...
Design a float for the parade

25

Ham It Up!

Cover the outside of a phonograph record holder with adhesive paper. Cover the inside of the phonograph record holder with felt. Place the following items in the record holder:

- scraps of felt
- felt tip pens
- scissors
- writing paper
- pencil
- drawing paper
- crayons
- task instructions

Print these directions on an index card:

Each student in the classroom is asked to present a puppet show at a specified time. Write a script to be used with your puppet show.

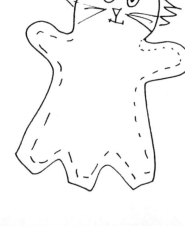

Print these directions on an index card:

Follow the directions and complete each task. Evaluate completed activities with the teacher.

26

Print these directions on an index card:

Use felt scraps and create the
puppets. The felt pens can be
used to make facial expressions
or outlines for clothing. Scenery
will be needed to complete the
puppet show. Design the
scenery from felt scraps.

Print these directions on an index card:

Provide music to be used between
scenes. Use a familiar tune and
write new words that relate to the
theme of the puppet show. Be
prepared to sing the song
or ask a friend to
help you sing.

Print these directions on an index card:

Each student will need a ticket
to attend the puppet show.
Design tickets and give each
student one.

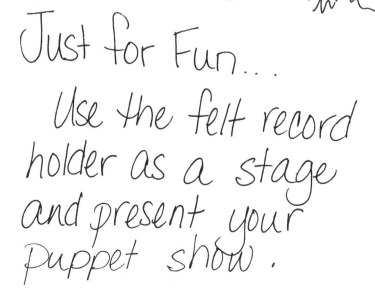

Just for Fun...
Use the felt record
holder as a stage
and present your
puppet show.

Handwriting HOTEL

Cut six large keys from poster board.
Attach the keys to a large key ring.
Punch a hole in writing and drawing
paper, attach yarn, and tie it to the
key ring. Use yarn and tie a pencil
and colored felt tip pens to the key ring.

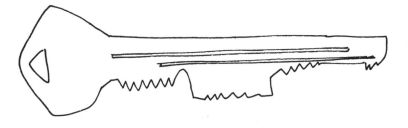

Print these directions on one of the keys:

Follow the directions and use the
drawing paper, pencil, and pens to
complete each task. Evaluate
completed activities with the teacher.

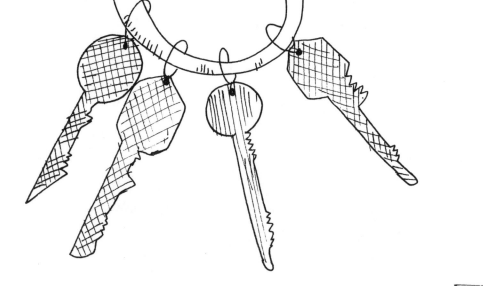

Print these directions on one of the keys:

You have been asked to design the
wallpaper in one room at Handwriting
Hotel. You must decide if the wallpaper design will be manuscript or
cursive letters of the alphabet. Be
sure to include both capitals and
small letters.

28

Print these directions on one of the keys:

The dining room of Handwriting Hotel has employed you to write the menus for one week. The manager says your handwriting is neat and this is why you got the job!

Print these directions on one of the keys:

Handwriting Hotel has a gift shop and book store. You are asked to make five signs for the Gift Shop and five book jackets for the Book Store.

Print these directions on one of the keys:

The Handwriting Hotel lobby has a guest register. Many famous people have spent the night at this hotel. Show how twenty-five guests may have signed the guest register. Be sure to add your signature to the list of guests!

Print these directions on one of the keys:

You decide to go swimming at Handwriting Hotel. While you are sitting in the sun beside the pool, you decide to write a poem in your nicest handwriting.

Just for Fun...
Make a film of your visit to Handwriting Hotel!

IGY WORDS

Place the following items in a styrofoam ice chest:

study guide on dictionary usage

> dictionary
> writing paper
> pencil
> kitchen timer
> task instructions

Draw and cut out a shape to resemble a soda pop bottle. Print these directions on the bottle and paste them on the ice chest:

Follow the directions and complete each task. Evaluate completed activities with the teacher.

Cut ten squares of tagboard to resemble pieces of bread. Cut twelve shapes from colored construction paper. Print the following words on the construction paper shapes:

lettuce	salami	peanut butter
ham	pickles	jelly
cheese	mustard	raisins
tuna	mayonnaise	tomatoes

Print these directions on a square of tagboard to resemble a sandwich:

Make an alphabetical order sandwich for the pic

Arrange the construction paper ingredients in alphabetical order and make four sandwiches. Now make one dagwood sandwich by arranging all the ingredients in alphabetical order.

Draw and cut out a shape to resemble
an ice chest. Print these directions
on the ice chest:

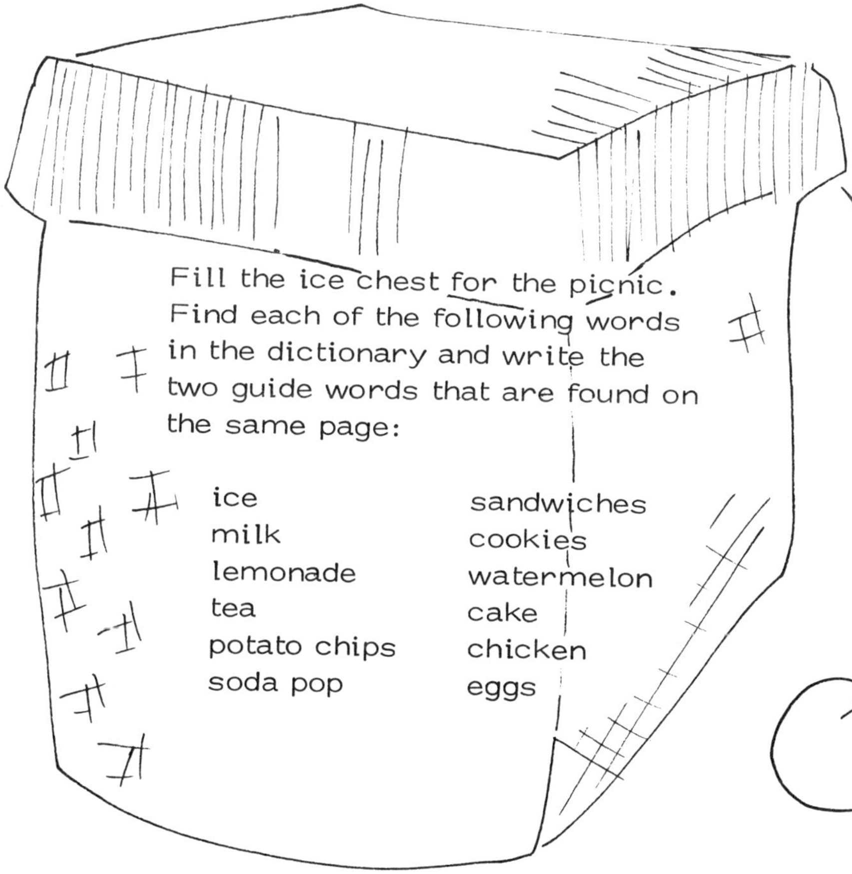

Fill the ice chest for the picnic.
Find each of the following words
in the dictionary and write the
two guide words that are found on
the same page:

ice	sandwiches
milk	cookies
lemonade	watermelon
tea	cake
potato chips	chicken
soda pop	eggs

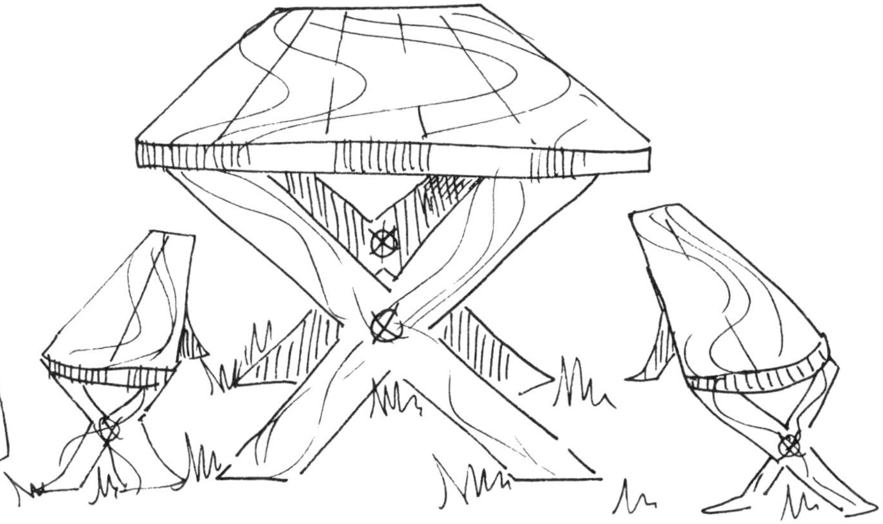

Draw and cut out a shape to resemble a picnic
table. Print forty words on the picnic table.
Print these directions on the picnic table:

After lunch, the picnickers decide
to play Dictionary Drill. Set the
timer for fifteen minutes. Look
up each word in the dictionary. See
how the word is pronounced and read
the definition of the word. Record the
amount of time it took you to play
                              Dictionary Drill.

Just for Fun...
Look up definitions for ten
words you would like to add
to your vocabulary.

31

LETTER LAND

Place the following items in a mailbox:

- writing paper
- drawing paper
- crayons
- pencil
- task instructions

Print these directions and place them in an envelope:

Follow the directions and use the paper and art materials to complete each task. Evaluate completed activities with the teacher. Share the pictures with your classmates.

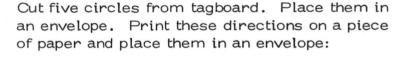

Cut five circles from tagboard. Place them in an envelope. Print these directions on a piece of paper and place them in an envelope:

Welcome to Letter Land! Hop on the bus for a tour of this unusual place. You will not need money for the bus ride but you are required to drop special tokens in the box. The bus driver will give you five tokens and you are to write one part of a letter and an example on each token. Enjoy your tour of Letter Land!

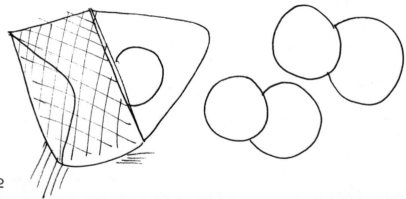

Print these directions on a piece of paper and place in an envelope:

The first stop on the tour is for lunch at Dewey's Delicatessen. The food looks delicious and the owner invites you to eat anything you wish. The waitress gives you a special check which says: No money is accepted for the meal. Instead, you must write a thank you letter.

Print these directions on a piece of paper and place in an envelope:

There will be a fifteen–minute stop at the Souvenir Shop. You select a gift to take home to your parents and one picture post card. You decide to write the picture post card before you pay for the gift and post card. As you leave, the cashier says, "No money is accepted, but you must design a postage stamp for each purchase."

Print these directions on a piece of paper and place them in an envelope:

You spend the night at Mail Motel. Letter Land has been so exciting you decide to write a letter to a friend telling all about your day's adventure. You want to include all the exciting things you have seen in Letter Land. The next morning the clerk tells you that you owe no money but would like for you to draw a mural showing the history of mail delivery.

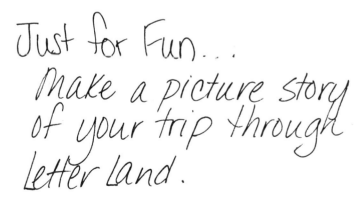

Just for Fun...
Make a picture story of your trip through Letter Land.

NEAT NOUNS

Place the following items in a shopping bag:

    writing paper
    white T-shirt
    masking tape
    colored construction
        paper
    scissors
    felt tip pen
    cassette tape recorder
    tape
    tagboard
    pencil
    crayons
    task instructions

Print these directions on a piece of construction paper and tape them on the shopping bag:

    Follow the directions and complete each task. Evaluate completed activities with the teacher.

Print these directions on a piece of construction paper and tape them on the T-shirt:

    Cut different shaped pieces of colored construction paper. Use a felt tip pen and draw a picture of a common noun on each shape of construction paper. Tape the pictures on the front and back of the T-shirt. Model the T-shirt for the class and wear it for the day!

34

Print these directions on an index card:

Cut a circle as large as a
phonograph record. Fill the
record with proper nouns.
Play the record by using a
familiar tune and using the
proper nouns as the words to
the tune. Tape the proper
noun song and share it with
the class!

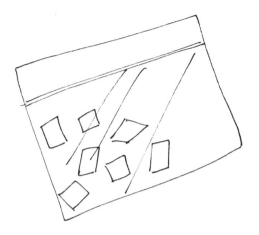

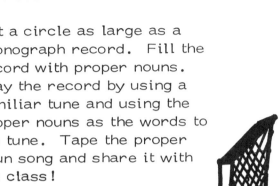

Print twenty nouns on small squares of
tagboard. Place the noun cards in a
plastic bag. Print these directions on a
piece of construction paper and place
in the plastic bag:

Write a creative story! Draw
a noun card and write a sentence.
Continue to draw a card and write
a sentence until the story is
complete.

Just for Fun...
Write three riddles. The
answer to each riddle
must be a noun.

Pillow Talk

Place the following items in a pillow case:

pillow
construction paper
paste
drawing paper
scissors
tape
cassette tape
  recorder
writing paper
pencil
crayons
task instructions

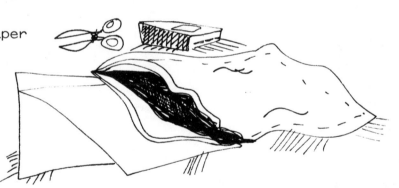

Print these directions on an index card:

Find a quiet corner in the classroom. Take everything
out of the pillow case except the pillow. Follow the
directions and complete each task. Evaluate completed
activities with the teacher.

Print these directions on an index card:

Make yourself comfort-
able with the pillow but
don't go to sleep! Close your
eyes and take an imaginary trip.
Now open your eyes and transfer
the imaginary trip to paper by
writing a story. Underline each
verb. Use the tape recorder and
tape your story. Share the
taped story with the class and
ask your classmates to identify
each verb.

Print fifteen present or past tense verbs and fifteen past participle verbs on an index card. (Example: go, eaten, etc.) Print these directions on the back of the index card:

Make a verb "patchwork" quilt. Read each verb on the index card. If the verb must have a helping word when used in a sentence, cut a shape from red construction paper. Write the verb on the shape. If the verb does not need a helping word when used in a sentence, cut a shape from blue construction paper. Write the verb on the shape. Design a verb "patch-work" quilt by pasting the shapes on a piece of drawing paper.

Cut twenty circles from tagboard. Print singular or simple verbs on ten circles. (Example: eat – run) Print plural verbs on ten circles. (Example: eats – runs) Print these directions on an index card:

Write a sentence with each verb. How does the subject change when a singular or plural verb is used?

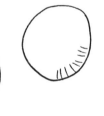

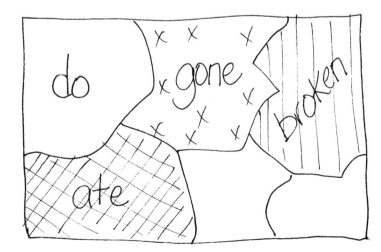

Just for Fun...

Illustrate six action verbs.

Plural Purse

Place the following items in a purse:

drawing paper	crayons
writing paper	study guide
pencil	task instructions

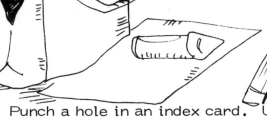

Punch a hole in an index card. Use yarn and tie the index card to the purse handle. Print these directions on the index card:

Follow the directions and complete each task. Evaluate completed activities with the teacher.

Draw or cut pictures from magazines of singular objects. Paste the pictures on small squares of tagboard. Place the picture cards in a plastic bag. Print these directions on a piece of colored construction paper and place them in the plastic bag:

Write the plural word for each picture.
Write a sentence using each plural word.

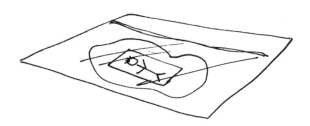

Print thirty words that have plural forms on small tagboard squares. Enlarge the clown and print these directions on the clown's back:

Read each word and make the word plural by placing it in the correct pocket.

Print these directions on an index card:

Use the clown activity word cards. Write the plural for each word. After each plural word, write the rule used to form the plural.

Example: church — churches
(The singular word ends in "ch" and "es" is added to make the word plural.)

Just for Fun...
Draw pictures showing the singular and plural of six words.

Pronoun Party

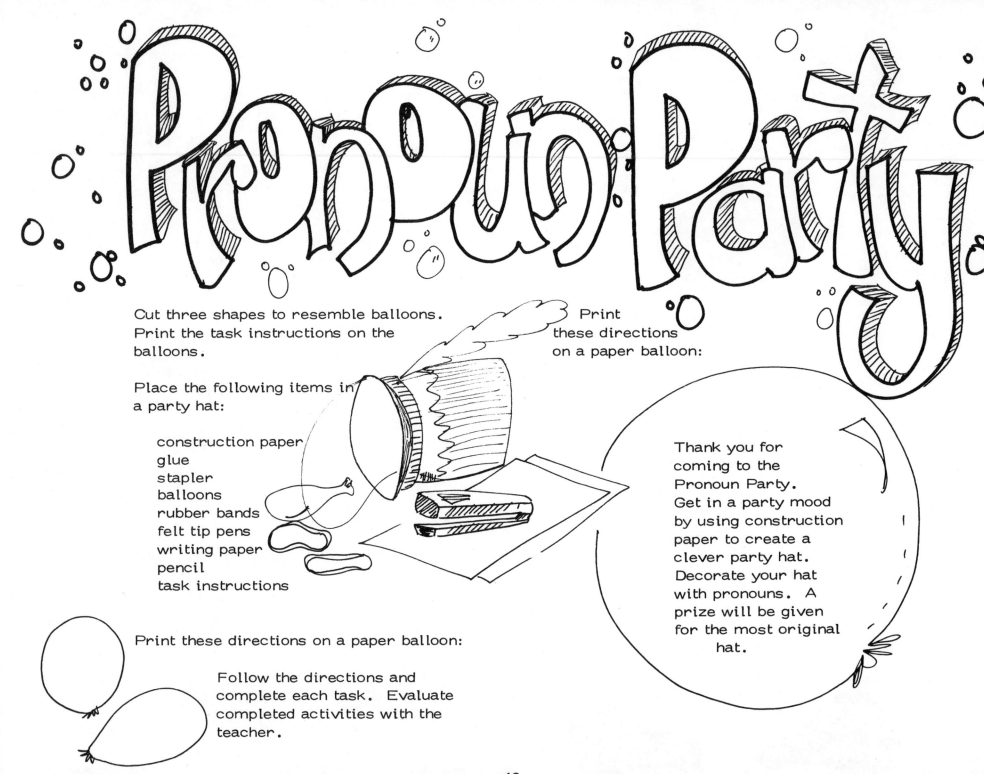

Cut three shapes to resemble balloons. Print the task instructions on the balloons.

Place the following items in a party hat:

    construction paper
    glue
    stapler
    balloons
    rubber bands
    felt tip pens
    writing paper
    pencil
    task instructions

Print these directions on a paper balloon:

    Follow the directions and complete each task. Evaluate completed activities with the teacher.

Print these directions on a paper balloon:

    Thank you for coming to the Pronoun Party. Get in a party mood by using construction paper to create a clever party hat. Decorate your hat with pronouns. A prize will be given for the most original hat.

Print these directions on a paper balloon:

The first game to be played at the Pronoun Party is "Balloon Juggling". Blow up three balloons and tie the ends with a rubber band. Use a felt tip pen and write personal pronouns on one balloon, indefinite pronouns on one balloon, and possessive pronouns on one balloon. Now try to juggle the balloons. If a balloon falls to the floor, you must write a sentence using one of the pronouns written on the balloon. Continue the game until you think you have mastered "Balloon Juggling".

Enlarge the game board. Print these directions on the back of the game board:

Enter the "Pin the Pronoun" contest. Close your eyes and point to any place in the picture. If your finger is closer to the word "personal" you must write a personal pronoun on a piece of construction paper and tape it to the picture, etc. Each pronoun is worth five points. If you write a sentence with the pronoun, you receive five more points. Total your score.

Just for fun...
Plan another game to play at the Pronoun Party.

41

Secret Syllables

Place the following items in a desk drawer:

tape   crayons
cassette tape   construction paper
    recorder   paste
writing paper   task instructions
pencil

Print these directions on a piece of colored construction paper and tape them on the drawer:

Follow the directions and complete each task. Evaluate completed activities with the teacher.

Select fifty words with different numbers of syllables and tape them. Print these directions on a piece of colored poster board:

Number your paper from 1 – 50. Listen to the tape and write the number of syllables each word contains.

automobile

Enlarge the puzzle. Print these directions on the back of the puzzle:

Color the one-syllable words red.
Color the two-syllable words green.
Color the three-syllable words yellow.

puzzle write sense these
desk favor read please
familiar social design printed
encourage music
neighbor word astronaut
creative cute or activity
reward disagree

Print these directions on a piece of colored construction paper:

Make a syllable bracelet. Cut strips of construction paper. Write a one-syllable word on the first strip of paper. Glue the ends of the strip. Write a two-syllable word on the second strip of paper. Attach it to the first strip to form a chain. Write a three-syllable word on the third strip of paper. Add the strip of paper to the chain. Write a four-syllable word to the fourth strip of paper. Add the strip of paper to the chain. Continue with a one-syllable word, etc. until the chain is complete. Enjoy wearing the bracelet.

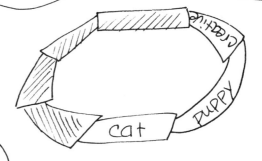

Just for Fun...
Write the name of each student in the class. Write the number of syllables in each name.

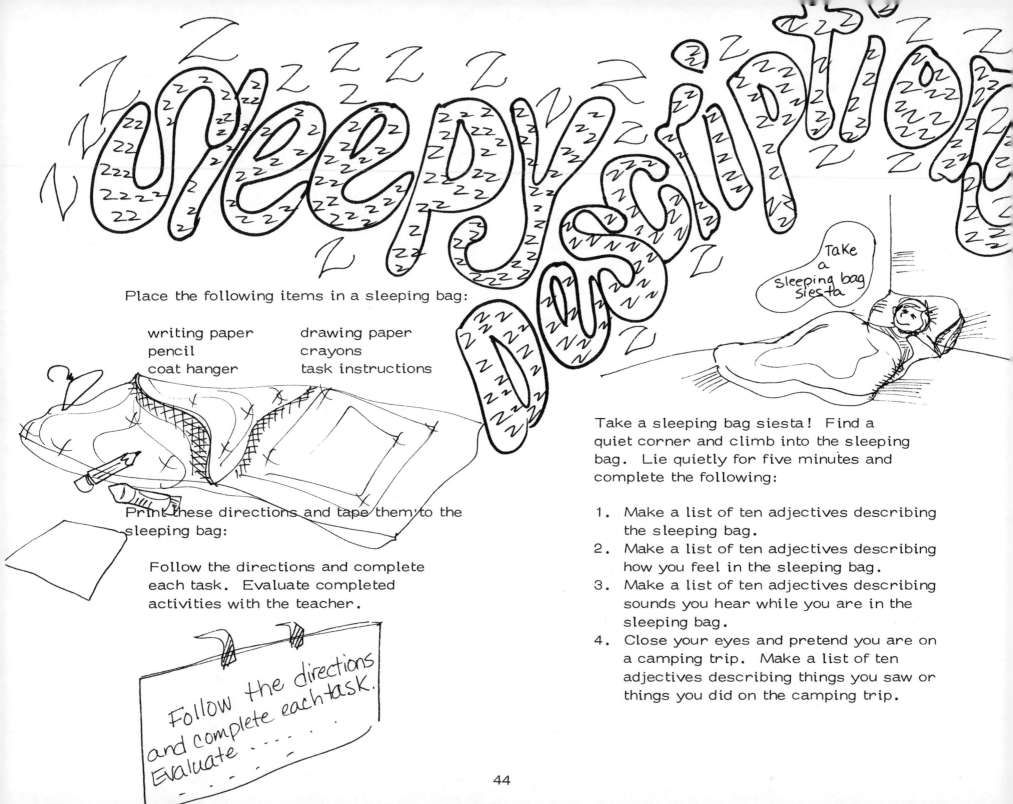

Sleepy Description

Place the following items in a sleeping bag:

writing paper   drawing paper
pencil   crayons
coat hanger   task instructions

Print these directions and tape them to the sleeping bag:

Follow the directions and complete each task. Evaluate completed activities with the teacher.

Follow the directions and complete each task. Evaluate . . . . .

Take a sleeping bag siesta

Take a sleeping bag siesta! Find a quiet corner and climb into the sleeping bag. Lie quietly for five minutes and complete the following:

1. Make a list of ten adjectives describing the sleeping bag.
2. Make a list of ten adjectives describing how you feel in the sleeping bag.
3. Make a list of ten adjectives describing sounds you hear while you are in the sleeping bag.
4. Close your eyes and pretend you are on a camping trip. Make a list of ten adjectives describing things you saw or things you did on the camping trip.

Print twenty nouns on small squares of tagboard. Place the noun cards in a plastic bag. Print these directions on an index card:

Shuffle the noun cards and place them face down. Draw one card and write at least three adjectives that describe the noun.

Example: man – tall–hungry–handsome

Continue until all the noun cards have been used.

dog
hat
house
car

Print these directions on an index card and attach it to a wire coat hanger:

Make an adjective mobile. Draw, color, and cut out a large picture of an animal, food, game, person, or other object that you would associate with a camping trip and tie it to the coat hanger. Draw and color descriptive pictures of the same object. Cut the pictures out and tie to the coat hanger to complete the mobile.

Example: picture of a cat

picture of a black cat
picture of a hungry cat (cat eating)
picture of a playful cat (cat playing)

Just for Fun...
Invent a new game to play on the camping trip.

45

Place the following items in a
large glass jar:

    writing paper
    pencil
    candy treat
    task instructions

Draw and cut out twenty-six shapes to
resemble lollipops. Print a letter of the
alphabet on each lollipop. Draw and cut
out one large lollipop and print these directions
on it:

    Draw a picture that begins with
    each letter on the lollipops.

Print these directions on the jar lid:

    Do these activities.
    (Be prepared to help
    read the task directions.)

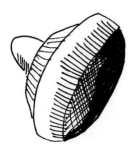

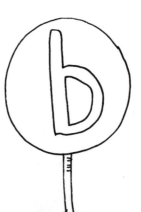

Draw and cut out fifteen shapes to resemble candy canes. Draw a stick figure or a symbol on one side of the candy cane to represent the following words:

run	jump	dance
skip	clap	dig
smile	crawl	eat
hop	wink	read
wave	walk	write

Print the word that matches the stick figure or symbol on the back of the candy cane. Print these directions on a large candy cane:

Look at each candy cane. Tell what each stick figure or symbol means. Read the word on the back of the candy cane.

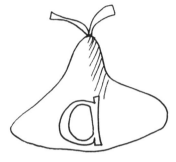

Draw and cut out fifty-two shapes to resemble candy kisses. Print the capital letters of the alphabet on twenty-six kisses. Print the small letters of the alphabet on twenty-six kisses. Place the kisses in a plastic bag.

Print these directions on a large candy kiss:

Match the capital letters with the small letters.

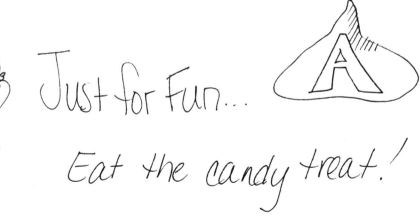

Just for Fun...

Eat the candy treat!

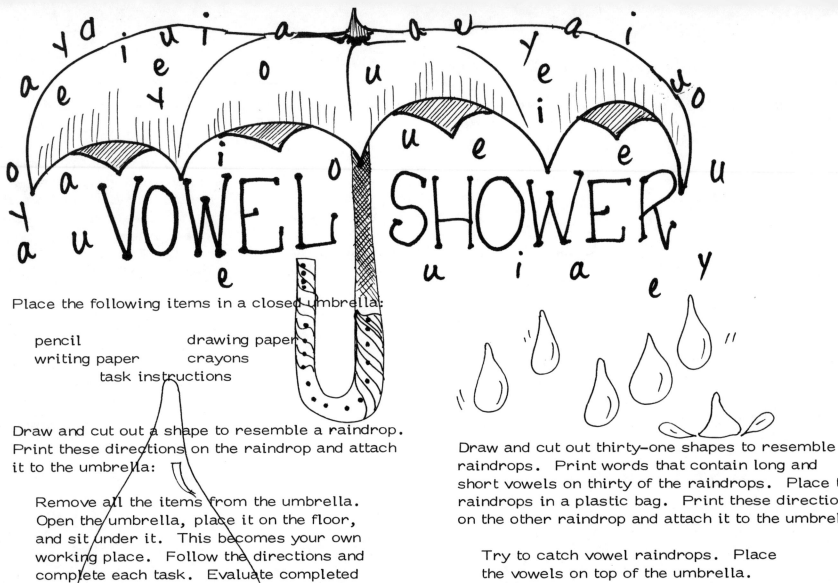

VOWEL SHOWER

Place the following items in a closed umbrella:

pencil   drawing paper
writing paper   crayons
     task instructions

Draw and cut out a shape to resemble a raindrop.
Print these directions on the raindrop and attach
it to the umbrella:

Remove all the items from the umbrella.
Open the umbrella, place it on the floor,
and sit under it. This becomes your own
working place. Follow the directions and
complete each task. Evaluate completed
activities with the teacher.

Draw and cut out thirty-one shapes to resemble
raindrops. Print words that contain long and
short vowels on thirty of the raindrops. Place the
raindrops in a plastic bag. Print these directions
on the other raindrop and attach it to the umbrella:

Try to catch vowel raindrops. Place
the vowels on top of the umbrella.
Catch the raindrops as they fall on
the floor. Write each word and
mark the word with a long or short
vowel sign.

48

Draw and cut out a shape to resemble a raindrop.
Print these directions on the raindrop and attach
it to the umbrella:

You have been employed as a fashion
designer. Create a new rain outfit.
Cover the outfit by writing words that
contain long and short vowels. Circle
the words that contain long vowels with
a blue crayon. Draw a red line under
the words that contain a short vowel.

chat hate hut
Key ice
age fill let
hit bat write
please side fat give tub hop
each Knead cup cute
hope fade male egg
stuck twice raise
place

Enlarge the picture and print these directions
on the back of the picture:

Peek inside a rain cloud! Use a blue
crayon and draw a raindrop shape
around each word that contains a long
vowel sound. Use a black crayon and
draw a raindrop shape around each
word that contains a short vowel sound.

Just for Fun...

Write a story, song,
or poem about a rainy
day. Illustrate your
creation.

49

Notes

Paint a hat box with red, white, and blue tempera paint to resemble a ballot box. Place the following items in the "ballot box":

cassette tape	tape recorder
writing paper	pencil
drawing paper	felt tip pen
crayons	shelf paper

task instructions

Use a black felt marker and print the following directions on the inside of the top of the "ballot box":

Follow the directions and complete each task. Evaluate completed activities with the teacher. Plan a mock election in the classroom.

MAYOR for a DAY.....

You have been nominated for the office of mayor.....

VOTE

Draw and cut out a campaign button. Print the following directions on the campaign button:

You have been nominated for the office of mayor of your city or town. The newspaper has telephoned to request an article stating your reasons for wanting to become mayor, what you plan to do if elected, your qualifications for the job, and a short biographical sketch. The newspaper has also asked for a photograph. Prepare these two items to be delivered to the newspaper office for publication.

Print the following directions on
a piece of tagboard that resembles
a dollar bill:

Money is an important item
for election campaigns. You
are a candidate for senator
from your state. You decide
to have a dinner to raise money
for campaign expenses.
Careful planning must be done
for the event to be a success.
Follow each step in coordinating
the gala affair.

1. Decide where the event will be
    held.
2. Write a sample invitation.
3. Plan a menu to be served.
4. Describe the entertainment.
5. Plan the decorations.
6. Write a speech that you will
    deliver to influence people to
    vote for you.

Design a bumper sticker. Print the following
directions on the bumper sticker:

You are campaigning for the office of
President of the United States.
Television is a means of communication
you have decided to use to reach the
most people. Write a television address
that explains the platform you will support
if elected President. Tape the speech
and use shelf paper to prepare a video
presentation to be shown on a nationwide
television broadcast.

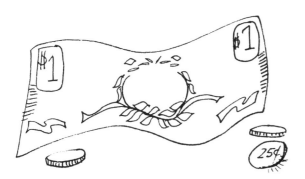

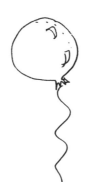

Just for Fun.....
Write a jingle to be used
on the radio to persuade people
to vote for you.

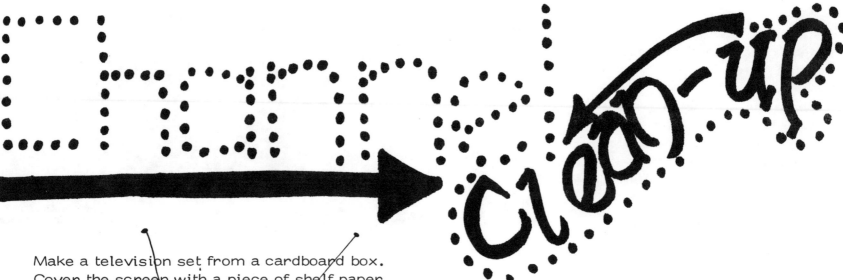

Channel → Clean-up

Make a television set from a cardboard box.
Cover the screen with a piece of shelf paper
and print the task directions on the screen.
Attach the shelf paper to dowel rods and
mount in the box. Place the following items
in the television set:

task instructions

tape	shelf paper
cassette tape recorder	pencil
writing paper	crayons

Print the following directions on the television
screen:

> Follow the directions and complete
> each task. Evaluate completed
> activities with the teacher. Share
> the television program with the class
> at a specified time.

Print the following directions on the television
screen:

> You are the director of Channel Clean-up.
> Next week has been proclaimed Ecology
> Week. You have been asked to produce
> a television program that will help
> people become more aware of our
> environment. The program will be
> thirty minutes with three commercial
> breaks. It is your responsibility to
> provide a name for the television program.
> Write the script for the ecology television
> program. When you have proofread the
> script, tape it for television use.

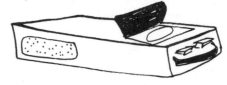

Print the following directions on the television screen:

The script for the ecology television program is complete and you must provide the pictures to be shown simultaneously with the tape. Use the shelf paper and draw pictures to correspond to the script. The pictures must cover the whole television screen, and this television program is in "living color".

Print the following directions on the television screen:

You are asked to participate in a panel discussion at the conclusion of the television program. This will be televised but the only preparation you must make is a list of questions about ecology that you would like to have answered. Prepare at least ten ecology questions that will help you become a better informed citizen.

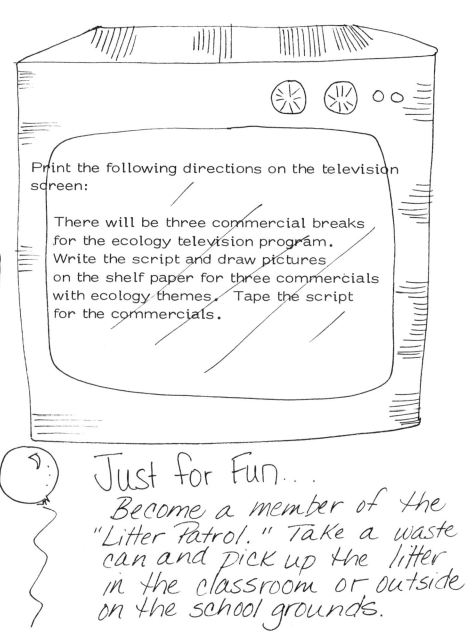

Print the following directions on the television screen:

There will be three commercial breaks for the ecology television program. Write the script and draw pictures on the shelf paper for three commercials with ecology themes. Tape the script for the commercials.

Just for Fun...
Become a member of the "Litter Patrol." Take a waste can and pick up the litter in the classroom or outside on the school grounds.

55

CLASSIFICATION CAN

Cover a large coffee can with attractive contact paper. Place the following items in the coffee can:

writing paper	scissors
drawing paper	paste
pencil	task materials and instructions
crayons	seed catalog

Print these directions and paste in the lid of the coffee can:

Follow the directions and complete the tasks. Evaluate completed activities with the teacher.

Cut a large leaf shape from colored construction paper. Print these directions on the leaf:

Take a walking field trip around the school. Collect the different leaves found on the trees growing on the school grounds. Bring the leaves back in the classroom. See how many ways you can group the leaves. (Example: size, shape, and color) List the different ways you group the leaves.

Cut pictures of different animals and paste them on pieces of poster board. Place the animal pictures in a plastic bag. Print these directions on an index card:

There are many characteristics which can be used to classify animals. (Example: number of feet; walk, fly, swim) Classify the animals into different groups. List the different groups in which you classified the animals.

Print these directions on a piece of colored construction paper:

Cut twelve different foods from the seed catalog. Classify the foods into different groups. Paste the pictures into groups. Label the pictures with the reason for the groupings. (Example: fruits – color)

Just for Fun...
See if you can classify the class into at least three different kinds of groups.

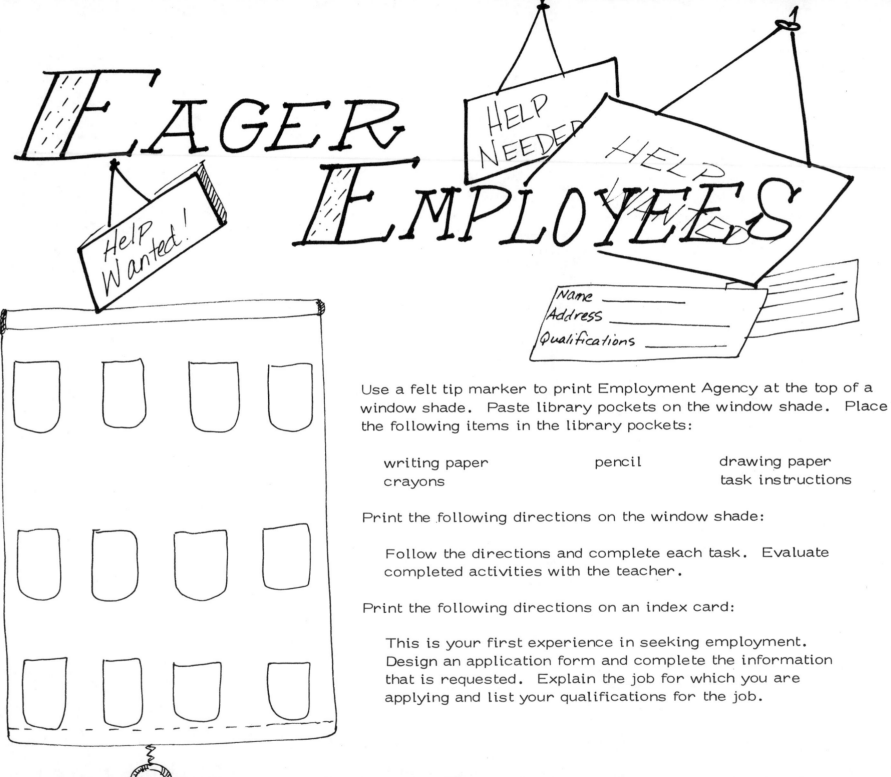

Eager Employees

Use a felt tip marker to print Employment Agency at the top of a window shade. Paste library pockets on the window shade. Place the following items in the library pockets:

writing paper	pencil	drawing paper
crayons		task instructions

Print the following directions on the window shade:

Follow the directions and complete each task. Evaluate completed activities with the teacher.

Print the following directions on an index card:

This is your first experience in seeking employment. Design an application form and complete the information that is requested. Explain the job for which you are applying and list your qualifications for the job.

Print the following directions on an index card:

A job description is an explanation of a certain occupation. Write three job descriptions that you feel you are qualified to perform.

Print the following directions on an index card:

The employment agency has requested an interview with you. Make a list of questions that could be asked during the interview. Describe the appropriate clothing to be worn for the interview.

Print the following directions on an index card:

Write a telephone dialogue between an interviewer in an employment agency and yourself as a job applicant.

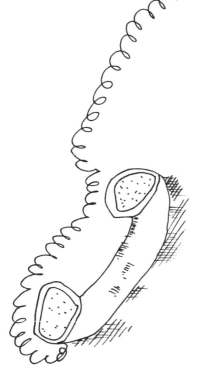

Just for Fun.....
Congratulations! You were hired for the job of your choice. Draw a picture of what you will buy with your first pay check.

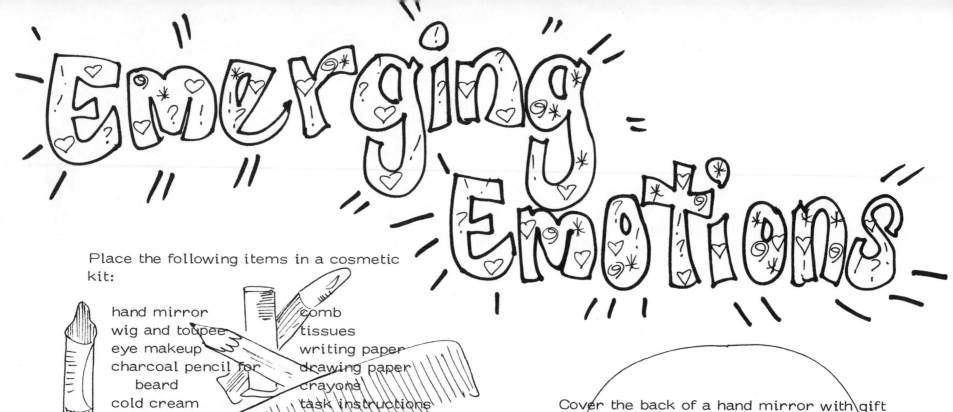

Emerging Emotions

Place the following items in a cosmetic kit:

hand mirror   comb
wig and toupee   tissues
eye makeup   writing paper
charcoal pencil for   drawing paper
    beard   crayons
cold cream   task instructions
lipstick

Print the following directions on a piece of construction paper and tape to the outside of the make-up bag:

Follow the directions and complete each task. Evaluate completed activities with the teacher.

Cover the back of a hand mirror with gift wrapping paper. Print these directions on the gift wrapping paper:

Self-concept is the way you feel about yourself. Look in the mirrow, and write a paragraph expressing how you feel about yourself. How do your friends perceive you? Look in the mirror again and write a paragraph that explains how you think other people perceive you.

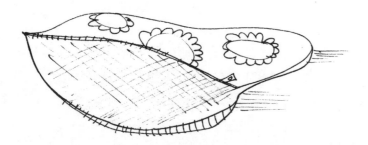

Print the following words on small squares of tagboard:

happiness	hate	fear
love	anxiety	sadness
anger	disappointment	frustration

Place the words in an envelope. Print these directions on the envelope:

Shuffle the cards. Draw one card and read the word. Look in the mirror and show the facial expression of the emotion that is written on the card. Continue until all the emotion cards have been expressed.

Draw an outline of a face on a piece of tagboard. Print the following directions on the face:

Look in the mirror of the future! Use the wig or toupee and cosmetics to create the way you might look in twenty years. Will your appearance change the feelings about yourself? Write a story predicting your life situation in twenty years. Include in the story the changes in your self concept, your family, foods, friends, occupation, house, and recreation. Draw a portrait showing the way you will look in twenty years. Use the cold cream to cleanse your face.

Just for Fun....
Look carefully at the students in the classroom. List the different emotions that you identify from their facial expressions. Now look at your teacher!

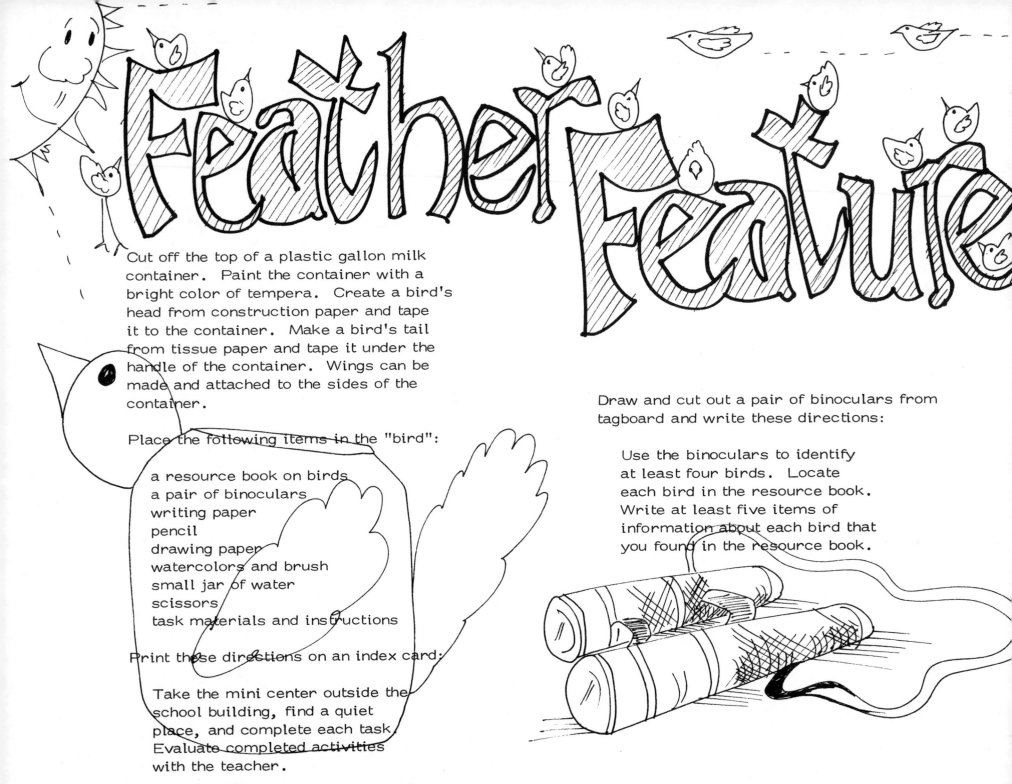

Feather Feature

Cut off the top of a plastic gallon milk container. Paint the container with a bright color of tempera. Create a bird's head from construction paper and tape it to the container. Make a bird's tail from tissue paper and tape it under the handle of the container. Wings can be made and attached to the sides of the container.

Place the following items in the "bird":

a resource book on birds
a pair of binoculars
writing paper
pencil
drawing paper
watercolors and brush
small jar of water
scissors
task materials and instructions

Print these directions on an index card:

Take the mini center outside the school building, find a quiet place, and complete each task. Evaluate completed activities with the teacher.

Draw and cut out a pair of binoculars from tagboard and write these directions:

Use the binoculars to identify at least four birds. Locate each bird in the resource book. Write at least five items of information about each bird that you found in the resource book.

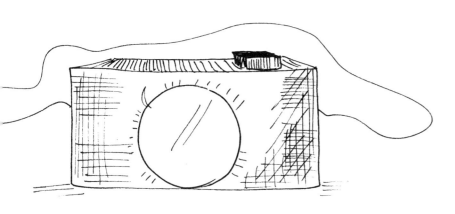

Use a piece of construction paper to make a camera, and print the following directions:

Take a picture of one of the birds with a magic camera. Use drawing paper and water colors to develop a picture of one of the birds that you identified. Cut out the bird and hang it on the mobile in the classroom.

Fold one 4 x 8" piece of construction paper in half. Write the word "Poems" on one side of the paper. Write the directions for the activity on the inside of the paper.

Sit quietly and watch a bird. Write a poem about the bird.

Just for Fun.... Write the conversation taking place in a bird's nest.

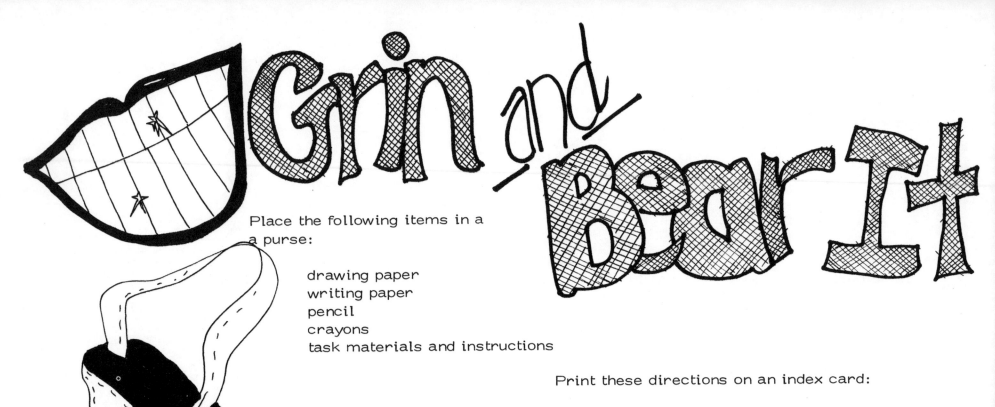

Grin and Bear It

Place the following items in a
a purse:

> drawing paper
> writing paper
> pencil
> crayons
> task materials and instructions

Print these directions on an index card:

> Use drawing paper and crayons to
> make a pictorial story showing
> how inflation has affected you and
> your family. Consider food,
> recreation, travel, clothes, school,
> and other family activities.

Print these directions and fasten in the purse:

> Follow the directions and complete the
> tasks. Evaluate completed activities
> with the teacher. Share pictorial story
> with the class.

Enlarge the budget form shown below on
a sheet of drawing paper:

Budget the family income for one month. Select a monthly income that you think is sufficient to provide the necessary essentials for your family

monthly income	
rent or house payment	
food	
utilities	
clothing	
transportation	
medical and dental bills	
insurance	
recreation	
savings	
other	
Total	
over or under budget	

Print these directions on a piece of colored construction paper:

You are a candidate for mayor of your city. Write an article that you want published in the newspaper stating your views on inflation and what you plan to do to halt it if you are elected.

Just for Fun...

Design a bumper sticker to help curb inflation.

Hit the Trail

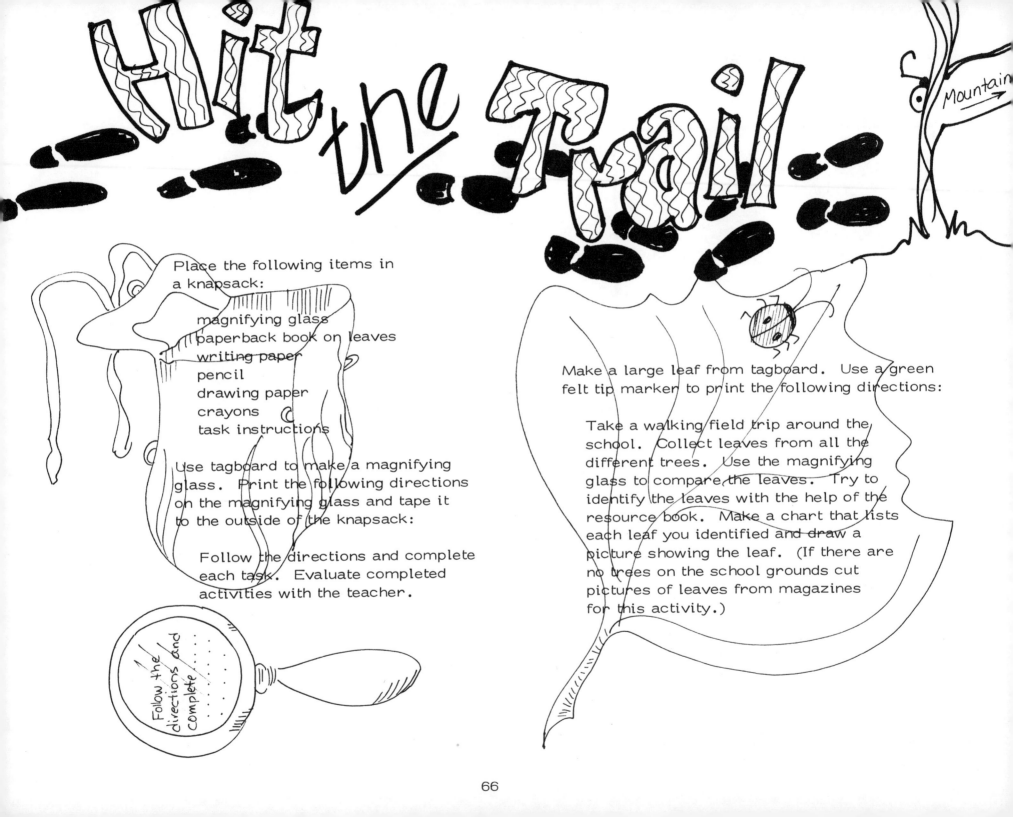

Mountain →

Place the following items in a knapsack:

    magnifying glass
    paperback book on leaves
    writing paper
    pencil
    drawing paper
    crayons
    task instructions

Use tagboard to make a magnifying glass. Print the following directions on the magnifying glass and tape it to the outside of the knapsack:

Follow the directions and complete each task. Evaluate completed activities with the teacher.

Follow the directions and complete .....

Make a large leaf from tagboard. Use a green felt tip marker to print the following directions:

Take a walking field trip around the school. Collect leaves from all the different trees. Use the magnifying glass to compare the leaves. Try to identify the leaves with the help of the resource book. Make a chart that lists each leaf you identified and draw a picture showing the leaf. (If there are no trees on the school grounds cut pictures of leaves from magazines for this activity.)

Cut a shape from tagboard that resembles an ear. Print the following directions on the ear:

Sit quietly and listen for different sounds. Write a list of all the sounds you hear. Place each sound in one of the following categories:

happy   working   unnecessary
sad   frightening   fun

Print the following directions on an index card:

All things are living or non-living. Find and list at least ten living and ten non-living things. Explain a characteristic that makes each thing living or non-living.

Draw a footprint on a piece of poster board. Cut it out and print the following directions on the footprint:

Look for different footprints and animal tracks. Examine them with a magnifying glass. Sketch the footprint or animal track and list the animal that you think made the footprint or track.

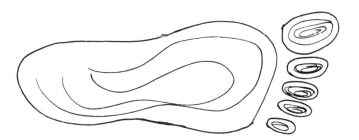

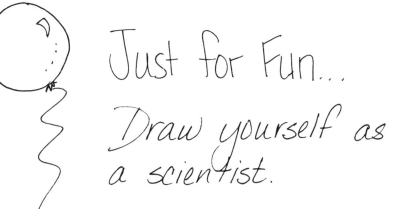

Just for Fun...
Draw yourself as a scientist.

magnificent MACHINES!

Place the following items in a tool box:

felt tip pen   pencil
scissors   envelope
stapler   paste
drawing paper   piece of tagboard 8 x 11"
crayons   modeling clay
task instructions and materials

Print the following directions on an index card and paste on the top of the tool box:

Follow the directions and complete each task. Evaluate completed activities with the teacher. Display your dictionary puzzle and machine.

Use a felt tip marker and print the following directions on an index card:

A publishing company has asked you to prepare a dictionary on simple machines. The six kinds of machines are: lever, wedge, wheel, ramp, pulley, and screw. The dictionary will contain a front and back cover, title page, and one page for each machine, or a total of nine pages. The machine pages must contain a definition of the machine and a picture showing an example of the machine. The dictionary is to be for sale soon. Good luck!

Print the following directions on an index card:

The sales of your dictionary are so great
that a game company has asked you to
create a machine puzzle. Draw and color
a large picture of any machine. Cut the
picture out, paste it on a piece of tagboard,
and cut it into puzzle pieces. Write one
of the following words on each puzzle piece:
lever, wedge, wheel, ramp, pulley, and
screw. Place the puzzle pieces in an
envelope. Invite a friend to put the puzzle
together by giving an example of the
machine that is written on the back of
each puzzle piece before adding the piece
to the puzzle.

Print the following directions on an index card:

You are becoming an authority on
machines. A machine manufacturing
company has awarded you a contract
to design and build a new kind of
machine. Use drawing paper and
sketch your new machine. When you
are satisfied with the sketch, use
modeling clay and create the machine.
Write a paragraph explaining the machine,
the different jobs it is capable of performing,
and how the machine will make the job
easier.

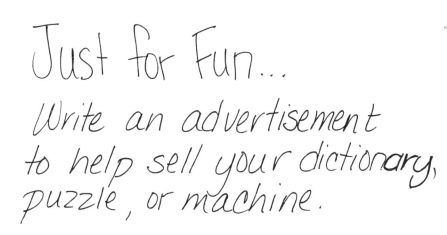

Just for fun...
Write an advertisement
to help sell your dictionary,
puzzle, or machine.

Matter Make-Up

Paste the task instructions on the sides of a waste basket. Place the following items in the waste basket:

glass bowl   modeling clay
glass   string
balloon   felt tip pen
plastic bag   chart tablet paper
rubber band   bottle of water
wire coat hanger   task instructions

Print the following directions on a piece of colored construction paper:

Follow the directions and complete each task. Evaluate completed activities with the teacher.

Print the following directions on a piece of colored construction paper:

You have been asked to appear on a television variety show to perform simple experiments to explain different properties of matter. The first experiment is to prove that air takes up space.

Fill the glass bowl almost full with water. Turn a glass upside down so that the bottom of the glass is touching the top of the water. Make a cue card for reference while you are performing on television. Write an explanation of why water does not get in the glass. Tip the glass over in the water. Explain on the cue card what happens to the air and the water.

70

Outline a piece of construction paper with a felt tip marker and print the following directions:

The second experiment proves that air changes shape.

Blow up a balloon. Tie a rubber band around the end of the balloon. Show the television audience the shape of the balloon. Carefully untie the balloon and let the air from the balloon out into a plastic bag. Close the plastic bag with a rubber band. Show the television audience the different shape of the air. Write a cue card that explains your experiment.

Use construction paper of a different color and print the following directions:

The third experiment proves that air has weight.

Suspend a wire coat hanger from the ceiling or doorway. Tie a balloon that has not been blown up on one end of the coat hanger. Add modeling clay to the other end of the coat hanger until the coat hanger balances. Untie the balloon and blow it up and attach the balloon to the coat hanger. Write a cue card to explain your experiment.

Just for Fun....
You are a success on television! Make a chart showing different kinds of matter to present at the end of the television program. Example: solid   liquid   gas
                    book   water   oxygen

news bag

Cut six inches from the top of a large grocery sack. Fold the six-inch strip and tape it on the bag to form a handle to make a "News Bag". Paint the "News Bag" with tempera paint. Place the following items in the "News Bag":

daily newspaper	drawing paper
writing paper	pencil
crayons	paste
task instructions	

Use a felt tip marker and print the following directions on the "News Bag":

Follow the directions and complete each task.
Evaluate completed activity with the teacher.

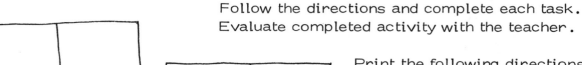

Print the following directions on the "News Bag":

Use the daily newspaper as a guide to read and find the following:

1. the headlines
2. a national news article
3. an international news article
4. a local news article
5. an editorial
6. the comics
7. the weather

72

Divide four pieces of 8-1/2 x 11" paper in half. Print the following directions on the sections of paper:

1. Write an article that might be found on the front page of a newspaper. Include in the article the answers to "who", "where", "when", "what", "why", and "how".
2. Draw an editorial cartoon.
3. Create your own comic strip.
4. Write your horoscope.
5. Report on a recent school sports event.
6. Make up some advertisements.
7. Draw a picture and write a caption that might be found in a newspaper.
8. Write an article and draw a picture that might be found on the society page.

Print the following directions on the "News Bag":

Use the daily newspaper and find an article that contains at least four paragraphs. Cut out the paragraph and paste it on a piece of drawing paper. Complete the following:

Paragraph I: Underline the subject of each sentence.

Paragraph II: Circle the verb in each sentence.

Paragraph III: Cross out each noun.

Paragraph IV: Draw a star around all the words that contain a consonant blend.

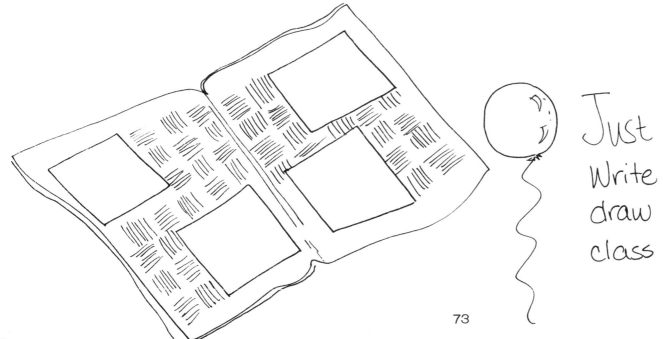

Just for fun....
Write an article and draw a picture for a class newspaper.

Planter's Punch

Place the following items in a clay flower pot:

a folded piece of white paper 24 x 36"
ruler
felt tip marker
pencil
crayons
writing paper
a resource book on vitamins and minerals
a gardening book
task materials and instructions

Cut a flower from construction paper. Print these directions on the flower and paste them on the flower pot:

Follow the directions and complete the tasks. Evaluate completed activities with the teacher.

Print the following directions on the back of the piece of white paper:

This piece of paper is a garden plot. Use the ruler and felt marker to draw twelve rows that are two inches apart. Draw and color the foods you will plant in each row. Write the directions for planting, how the plants will look, and how the plants will be harvested in the 2" space under each row in the garden.

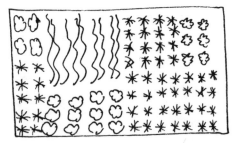

Make a pair of garden gloves by tracing two hands on tagboard. Print the following directions on the pair of gloves:

Take each food that was planted in the garden and make a list of the different ways the food can be eaten.

Example: carrots
(cooked – raw – juice)

Make up a recipe using one of the foods that was planted in the garden. Use crayons to show your creation.

Create a garden tool from tagboard. Print the following directions on the tool:

Use the resource book and list the vitamins and minerals in each food that were planted in the garden.

Just for Fun...
Pretend that you are a seed. Write a story telling about your life.

rainbow roundup

Paint a pizza box with bright
tempera paint. Cut a cardboard
pizza circle into four equal sections.
Paint each section a different color.
Place the following items in the pizza box:

color wheel   two 8 x 8" pieces of tagboard
water colors   plastic pill bottles
food coloring   3 x 2" strips of tagboard
crayons   drawing paper
compass   task instructions

Use a black felt tip pen and print these directions on
one section of the pizza circle:

Follow the directions and complete each
task. Evaluate completed activities with
the teacher.

Print these directions on one section of
the pizza circle:

Use the compass and draw a circle
on a piece of tagboard. Make a color wheel
by mixing food coloring with water in the
plastic pill bottles and placing the bottles
on the circle.

Print these directions on one section of
the pizza circle:

Take a poll of all the colors worn
by your classmates. Use the strips
of tagboard and crayons and color
one strip for each color that is worn.
Use the compass and draw a circle
on a piece of tagboard. Arrange the
colored tagboard strips to form a
color wheel. Are all the colors
represented?

Print these directions on one section of the
pizza circle:

Colors remind you of certain emotions.
Read each word and use watercolors to
show the color that reminds you of each
emotion.

sad	disappointment
angry	lonely
love	frustration
happy	hate
anxious	fear

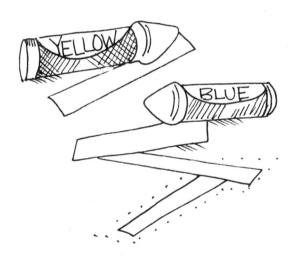

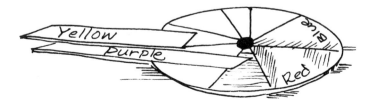

Just for Fun....
Use water colors to
paint a fun picture!
See how many different
colors you can include in
the picture.

Recipe Writers

Place the following items in a recipe box:

    drawing
      paper
    crayons
    writing paper
    pencil
    stapler
    task instructions

Print these directions on an index card:

Follow the directions and complete each task. Evaluate completed activities with the teacher.

Print these directions on an index card:

A large publishing company has asked you to compile a cookbook. However, this cookbook does not contain recipes involving food. It contains value recipes. Design the front and back covers for the cookbook. Give the cookbook a title. Don't forget to include your name as the author.

Print these directions on an index card:

The cookbook is divided into two sections. The first section includes the following values:

happiness
success
friendship
health
love
wealth

What are your ingredients for each value? Write a recipe for each of the values. Each recipe should become one page in the cookbook.

Print these directions on an index card:

The second section of the cookbook includes the following values or ideas:

overcoming prejudices
using time wisely
trying not to worry
becoming a better student
breaking a bad habit

Write a recipe for each of the ideas. Staple the cookbook together and share it with the class.

love

health

happiness

success

Just for Fun...
Illustrate your cookbook.

Topography Talent

Place the following items in a large plastic bucket:

pencil   poster board (8 x 11")
drawing paper   plastic wrap
felt tip pen   tempera paint (green and brown)
crayons   aluminum foil
modeling clay   resource book that includes
task instructions   information about the state
                in which you are living

Print these directions on colored construction paper and paste on the outside of the bucket:

Follow the directions and complete each task. Evaluate completed activities with the teacher. Share the maps with the class at a specified time.

Print these directions on a piece of colored construction paper. Label the directions Assignment I. Paste the directions on the outside of the bucket.

Congratulations! You are now an employee of Topography Talent, Inc. Your first assignment is to draw a map of your classroom. Use a pencil to sketch the map on a piece of drawing paper. Complete the map by using a felt tip marker to complete the drawing.

Print these directions on construction paper of another color. Label the directions Assignment II and paste them on the outside of the bucket.

Topography Talent, Inc. is pleased with the first map you drew. You are receiving a promotion! Your next assignment is to draw a map of your neighborhood. Use crayons to show the details and label the map for easy reading.

School

Shopping Center

Cut out the shape of the state in which you live. Print these directions on the "state". Label the directions Assignment III. Paste the directions on the outside of the bucket.

You have been chosen to be the supervisor of the state map section of Topography Talent, Inc. It is your responsibility to make a map of your state. The resource book will be your guide. Use clay to make the map. Plastic wrap, aluminum foil, and tempera paint can be used to show the different land forms. Place the map on the poster board.

CLAY

TENN.

Just for Fun......

Hide an object in the classroom. Make a map leading to the hidden object. Ask a friend to follow the map and find the "secret treasure."

transportation tipsters

Place the following items in a toy wagon:

colored chalk   mural paper
kitchen timer   writing paper
pencil   crayons
task materials and instructions

Draw and cut out a cardboard car. Print
the following directions on it.

Follow the directions and complete
each task. Evaluate completed
activities with the teacher.
Display your mural.

Draw and cut out a cardboard ship. Print
these directions on it:

The Department of Transportation
has commissioned you to create
a mural depicting the history of
transportation. The mural will be
displayed in the school lobby. Use
colored chalk to draw the mural.

Cut small squares of tagboard. Print the following words on the tagboard squares:

Indian	Eskimo
Viking	snow
ice	sailor
child	Pilgrim
soldier	astronaut
pilot	mail
underground	school
shoes	parents
balloon	desert

Place the tagboard squares in an envelope. Print these directions on the envelope:

Shuffle the word cards. Number a piece of writing paper from one to eighteen. Set the kitchen timer for five minutes. Draw a card and read the word. Write the means of transportation that the word suggests. (Example: engineer – train) Continue until all the word cards have been used. Record the amount of time it took for the activity.

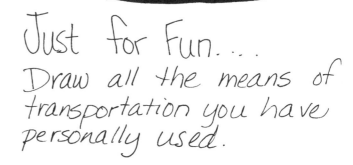

Use tagboard and outline a circle to resemble a crystal ball. Print the following directions on the crystal ball:

Transportation can be broadly categorized into three groups, past, present, and future. Select one category and write a report on all the means of transportation during that time period.

Just for Fun....
Draw all the means of transportation you have personally used.

Notes

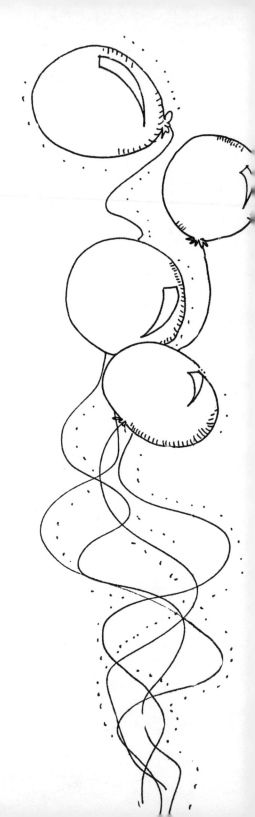

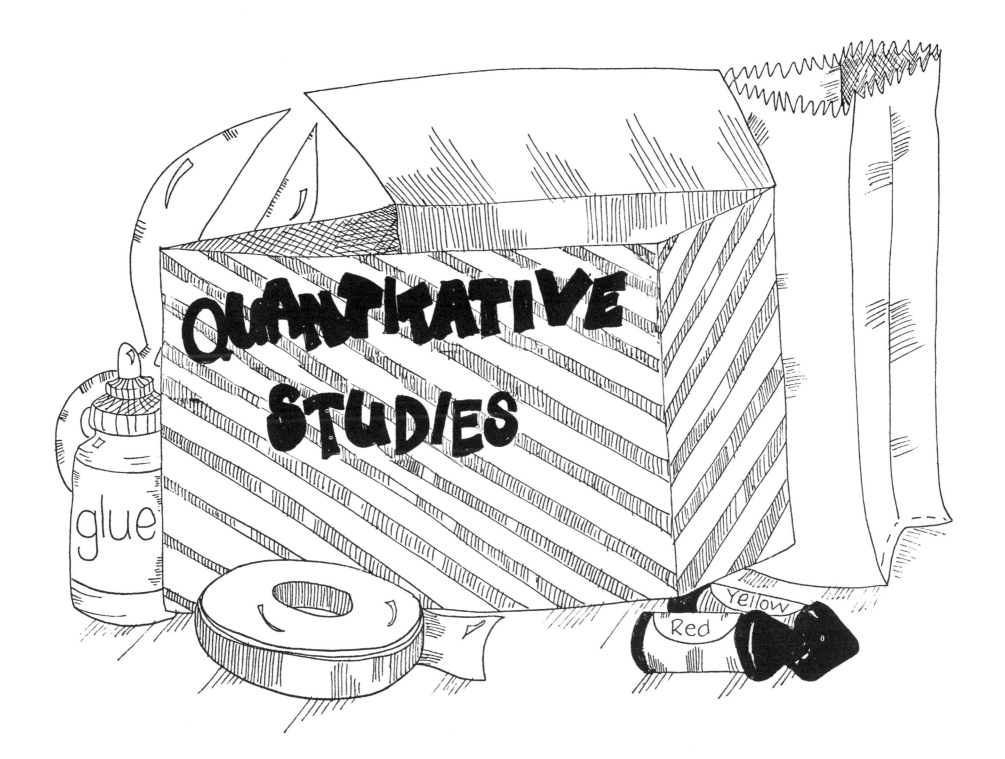

Write addition problems randomly on a white gift box large enough to hold a telephone directory and the other materials specified in the activities. Place all materials inside the box. Attach a pencil with a good eraser to the box with black yarn.

Print these directions on the inside of the box top:

Follow the directions and complete the tasks. Evaluate completed activities with the teacher.

Print these directions on a piece of colored construction paper. Paper clip the construction paper to a telephone directory.

Use the telephone directory to find these numbers:

your home telephone	a friend
school	a church
a bank	a grocery store
a drug store	a florist
a doctor	a dentist
a furniture store	a neighbor
television repair	fire department

Write an addition problem for each telephone number. Solve each problem. (Example: home telephone – 297 – 4467
2 + 9 + 7 + 4 + 4 + 6 + 7 = 39)

Enlarge the puzzle. Print these directions on the puzzle:

Addition facts are hidden in the puzzle. See how many you can find.

10	4	6	3	9	2	2	4
2	4	0	2	3	5	1	5
6	8	14	5	12	7	3	9
5	10	1	4	2	6	8	1
3	6	16	9	7	17	8	10
9	6	11	13	2	0	16	3
5	12	7	6	5	2	7	11
14	6	3	9	12	8	4	4
7	4	10	3	15	6	9	7
7	9	9	18	20	13	6	2

Cut the numbers 1 – 9 out of poster board. Laminate the numbers for durability. Print the following directions on an index card:

Arrange the numbers to form two digits and write ten addition problems. Solve the problems. Example:

$$\begin{array}{r} 43 \\ +\ 67 \\ \hline 110 \end{array}$$

Arrange the numbers to form three digits and write ten addition problems. Solve the problems. Example:

$$\begin{array}{r} 789 \\ +\ 123 \\ \hline 912 \end{array}$$

Place all activity materials in a snap top plastic bag.

Just for Fun......
Make up a page of addition problems for a friend to solve. Check the completed problems and return to your friend.

Paint storefronts on a long rectangular piece of tagboard to create an avenue setting. Paste a piece of paper behind the tagboard to form a pocket to hold the task instructions. Cut openings for the store doors and place the following items in the doors:

writing paper	catalog
pencil	task instructions

Print these directions on one of the store doors:

Follow the directions and complete each task. Evaluate completed activities with the teacher.

Cut fifty 1" squares. Print a number on each square. Place the numbered squares in an envelope. Print these directions on the envelope:

Shuffle the numbered squares. Draw three numbered squares and add the three numbers. Find the average of the three numbers by dividing the sum by 3. Continue to find the average of three numbered squares until all the squares have been used.

Use the class roll to list each student's weight, height, and number in family. Place the list in an envelope. Print the following directions on the envelope:

Find the average of the class weight, height, and number in family. Find the average of the girls' weight, height, and number in family. Find the average of the boys' weight, height, and number in family.

John Adams
Becky Burns
Carol Corn
David Dunn

Print these directions on an index card and attach it to a small catalog:

You have been selected to be a consumer reporter for the newspaper. Look in the catalog and find an item you would like to buy. Compare prices of the same item. Find the average price of the item. (Example: radio)

Prices of all the radios in the catalog –

$24.64 $25.87
 13.18   3⟌$77.61
 39.79
─────
$77.61

Continue until you find the average price of ten different items.

Just for fun....
Make a graph showing the average class weight, height, and number in family.

drummer's drill

Use tempera paint to paint an oatmeal box to resemble a drum. Place the following items in the drum:

kitchen timer
writing paper
pencil
tape
cassette tape recorder
task materials and instructions

Print these directions and paste in the top of the oatmeal box:

Follow the directions and complete each task. Evaluate completed activities with the teacher.

Cut twenty 3" squares from tagboard. Print an addition problem on each tagboard square. (The addition problems can be on different levels of difficulty.) Place the squares in a small box. Print these directions on the top of the box:

Shuffle the cards and place them face down. Set the timer for ten minutes. Draw one card, write, and solve the addition problem. Continue until all the problems have been solved. Record the length of time it took to complete the problems.

Cut forty circles from tagboard. Print a number on each circle. Place the circles in an envelope. Print these directions on the envelope:

Place the circles face down on a table, desk, or floor. Set the kitchen timer for ten minutes. Draw two circles. Write and solve a subtraction problem using the two numbers.

Example: 63   24   63
                         − 24
                         ____
                           39

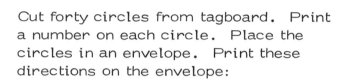

Continue until you have twenty subtraction problems solved. Record the length of time it took to complete the twenty subtraction problems.

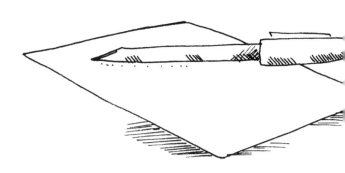

Use a felt tip pen and print all the multiplication and division facts on a piece of colored poster board. Provide an answer key. Print these directions on another piece of colored poster board:

Turn the tape recorder to "record". Read each multiplication or division fact and give the answer. When you have given the answers to all the facts, rewind the tape. Listen to the tape and check your answers with the answer key.

Just for Fun...
Write one addition, one subtraction, one multiplication, and one division problem. Set the Kitchen timer and see how fast you can solve the problems.

Kilometer Know-How

Place the following items in a toy car, truck, or bus:

  road map
  study guide explaining the conversion
    of miles to kilometers
  writing paper
  drawing paper
  crayons
  pencil
  task instructions

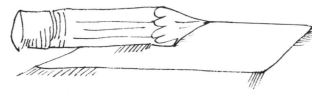

Print these directions on a piece of tagboard and tape it to the side of the toy car:

  Follow the directions and complete
  each task. Evaluate completed
  activities with the teacher.

Make a highway sign from tagboard and print these directions on the sign:

Read the study guide and change these miles to kilometers:

30 miles	26 miles
10 miles	50 miles
18 miles	3 miles
95 miles	42 miles
5 miles	88 miles
46 miles	2 miles

Make a highway sign from tagboard and print
these directions on the sign:

Use drawing paper and crayons to make
a highway sign showing each of the
following miles in kilometers. Make
it more interesting by inventing a name
of a town to add to the sign.

Example: Agenda – 22 miles – 35 kilometers

67 miles	40 miles
12 miles	4 miles
24 miles	36 miles

Print these directions on a piece of poster board :

Locate your home town on the road map
and plan a trip that will take you to a
city 300 miles from your home. List
each town or city that you will pass to
reach your destination. Convert the
miles between each town or city to
kilometers.

NASHVILLE
69 MILES
__ KILOMETERS

NEW YORK CITY
123 MILES
__ KILOMETERS

CHICAGO
82 MILES
__ KILOMETERS

Just for Fun......
Find the number of
Kilometers from your house
to school.

Use two rectangular pieces of felt to make a money bag. Add a drawstring and paint a dollar sign on the side of the money bag.

Place the following items in the money bag:

play money	scissors
food ads from newspaper	glue
drawing paper	pencil
writing paper	crayons
task instructions	

Print the following directions on an index card and paper clip to the money bag:

Complete the tasks and evaluate completed activities with the teacher.

Print the following directions on a piece of tagboard shaped like a dollar bill:

Show the coins and bills that make each of the following amounts of money:

$1.15	49¢	$1.19	43¢
28¢	58¢	99¢	$2.49
76¢	89¢	29¢	$6.18
$1.69	$3.98	67¢	18¢

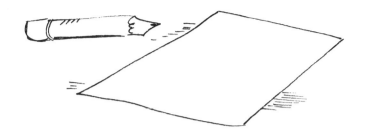

Print these directions on a piece of poster board:

You have purchased a building in a new shopping center. Decide what type of store you will open. Give the store a name. Show how the inside will look on drawing paper. Draw the objects for sale and list the price of each item. Use the play money to show how much each item will cost.

Print these directions on an index card:

You have won the "Shopper of the Week" award. Draw a large shopping cart on a piece of drawing paper. Cut out a food ad from the newspaper and paste it in the cart. Take the amount of money the food will cost and place it beside the shopping cart. When you have filled the shopping cart, write the total amount of money the food will cost under the shopping cart.

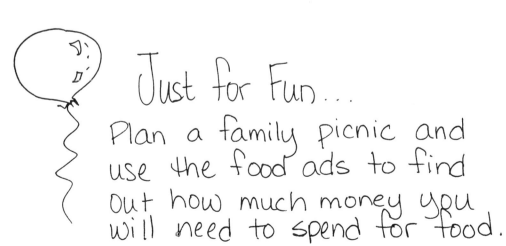

Just for Fun...
Plan a family picnic and use the food ads to find out how much money you will need to spend for food.

MYSTERY MANSION

Paint a square cardboard box to resemble a haunted mansion. Tape the top of the box together to form a roof. Cut a door large enough for the following items to be placed inside the house:

    outline of inside of house
    pencil
    crayons
    secret message key

Use a black felt marker and print these directions on the door of the house:

    Follow the directions and complete each task. Evaluate completed activities with the teacher.

Draw an outline of the inside of a house on a large piece of brown paper or shelf paper. Include at least three rooms.

Print these directions in the first room of the house:

Welcome to the haunted mansion! Don't be frightened! If you follow the directions you will be out of the house quickly. The room is filled with invisible division facts. Take the magic pencil and reveal the division facts. As you write, all of the invisible division facts will appear. When you finish, a door will open into the next room.

Print twenty division problems in the room.
(Example: 664 ÷ 8 =)
Print these directions in the second room:

The cobwebs and dust have covered
all the furniture, pictures, lamps,
books, and rugs. As you blow the
dust away, division problems will
become visible. The problems are
written on the furnishings. Solve
the problems and then draw the
furniture, pictures, lamps, books,
and rugs around the problems. When
you finish, a strange noise will
signal you to enter the next room.

Print these directions and problems in the
third room:

Solve the secret message and you will
be allowed to leave the haunted mansion.

186 ÷ 6 =	93 ÷ 3 =
384 ÷ 4 =	693 ÷ 7 =
250 ÷ 5 =	60 ÷ 3 =
36 ÷ 3 =	574 ÷ 7 =
100 ÷ 5 =	140 ÷ 7 =
99 ÷ 3 =	784 ÷ 8 =
344 ÷ 8 =	400 ÷ 8 =
828 ÷ 9 =	276 ÷ 3 =
80 ÷ 4 =	168 ÷ 4 =
492 ÷ 6 =	96 ÷ 6 =

180 ÷ 9 =

Make a key to solve the secret message:

A	B	C	D	E	F	G	H	I	J	K	L
43	99	5	56	20	13	85	92	50	24	96	42

M	N	O	P	Q	R	S	T	U	V	W	X
60	12	9	18	39	3	82	31	33	16	40	80

Y	Z
98	15

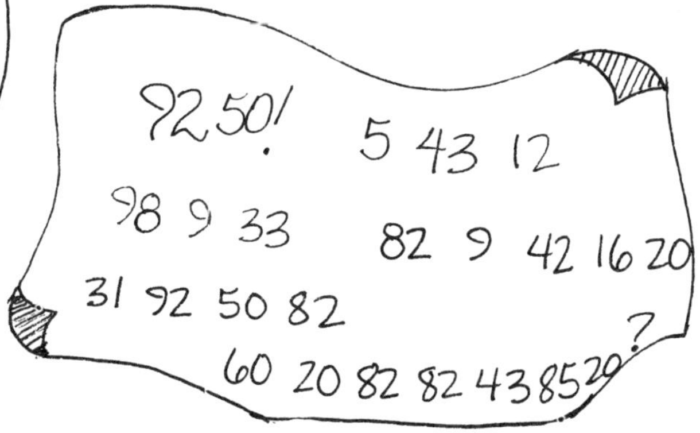

92 50!   5 43 12
98 9 33   82 9 42 16 20
31 92 50 82
60 20 82 82 43 85 20 ?

Just for Fun....
Use the key and make your
own secret message. Let a
friend solve the secret message.

97

PARTIAL PICNIC

Cover the inside and top of a cigar box with felt. Paint the outside of the cigar box with tempera paint to resemble a picnic basket. Place the following items in the picnic basket:

red felt apple	felt strips to make
felt pie	fractions
felt sandwich	scissors
felt quart of milk	drawing paper
felt numbers 1 – 8	pencil
crayons	task instructions and
	materials

Print these instructions on a cookie cut from brown construction paper:

Follow the directions and complete each task. Evaluate completed activities with the teacher.

Draw and cut out an apple from red construction paper. Print the task directions on the apple.

It's time for a picnic. Four people will share the apple equally. Use the scissors and cut the apple to show how much each person will receive. Use the felt numbers to show the fraction that represents each piece of apple. Place the apple and fraction on the lid of the cigar box.

Print these directions on a square piece of poster board. Color the square to resemble a sandwich.

Cut the sandwich in half to share with a friend. Place the two halves and the fraction that represents each piece of sandwich on the lid of the cigar box.

Draw, color, and cut out a pie from tagboard. Print these directions on an index card:

> Eight people are invited to eat the pie. Cut the pie into eight equal pieces. Place the pie pieces and the fraction that represents each piece of pie on the lid of the cigar box.

Draw and cut out a quart of milk from white drawing paper. Print these directions on an index card:

> There are four cups in one quart. Only three cups of milk are drunk at the picnic. Use the scissors and show how much milk was drunk and how much is remaining. Place the milk and the fraction showing how much milk was drunk in the lid of the cigar box.

Just for Fun....
Draw and color an object that can be divided into each of the fractions that were shown with the apple, sandwich, pie, and milk. Write the fraction beside each object.

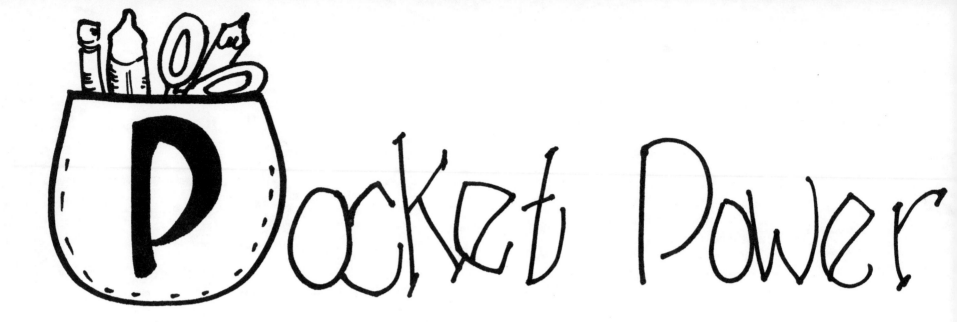

Pocket Power

Use an overhead projector to enlarge the kangaroo on a piece of poster board. Paste a piece of paper on the back of the kangaroo to form a pocket. Print these directions on the pocket:

Follow the directions and complete each task. Evaluate completed activities with the teacher.

Paint the kangaroo a bright color of tempera paint. Place the following items in the kangaroo's pocket:

ruler showing inches and centimeters
pencil
writing paper
cardboard clock
task envelopes

Print ten story problems on ten strips of tagboard. Print ten answers on ten strips of tagboard. Some answers should be correct and others estimates. Place the problems and answers in an envelope. Print the following instructions on the envelope:

Read the story problems and try to match an answer with each problem. Then solve each problem on paper and decide if the answer is an exact or an estimated answer.

Print the following words on square pieces of tagboard:

desk	wastebasket
chair	book
pencil	teacher
friend	bookcase
pencil sharpener	table
chalk board	door
	window

Place the words in an envelope. Print these instructions on the envelope:

Read the cards and write the estimated height of each object in inches, centimeters, feet, yards, and meters. Then use the ruler to find the exact measurement of each object. Compare the estimated answer with the exact measurement.

Cut ten circles and draw a clock on each circle. Print one of the following times on each clock:

6:50 – 8:15	4:19 – 7:55
3:05 – 12:20	10:10 – 3:45
12:25 – 1:05	9:30 – 2:15
7:40 – 9:18	8:10 – 2:45
1:35 – 11:45	11:17 – 1:38

Place the clocks in an envelope. Print these instructions on the envelope:

Write an estimate of how many hours and minutes are between the two times on each clock. Then use the clocks to help you write the exact number of hours and minutes between the two times on the clock.

Just for Fun...
Estimate the weight of five of your classmates. Ask the classmates for their exact weight.

ROCKET REVIEW

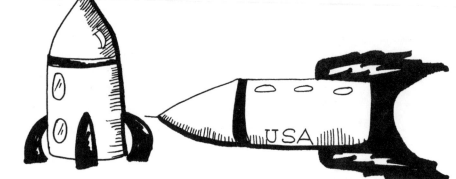

Paint an oatmeal box to resemble a rocket. Place the following items in the "rocket":

tape
cassette tape recorder
writing paper
drawing paper
pencil
crayons

Use a red felt tip pen to print the following directions on the lid of the "rocket":

Listen to the tape and follow the directions. Evaluate completed work with the teacher and share your rocket trip picture.

Tape the following story problems. Repeat each problem two times and allow time for the student to complete each problem. Provide an answer key for checking answers.

"Welcome aboard! You are one of the first passengers on a rocket that will journey into space. Since the rocket is small, you are only allowed to bring a pencil, crayons, writing paper, and drawing paper on the trip. Look out the rocket window, listen carefully, and use the writing paper to solve each story problem. Number the problems as you hear the countdown.

10. Check the blinking lights before you blast off. There are six rows with three in each row of red lights and three rows with four in each row of green lights. How many lights are blinking?

9. The control room is sending a signal. You should hear twenty-one "beeps" before blast-off. You have heard thirteen "beeps". How many more "beeps" should you hear?

8. The fuel gauge says you will use 378 gallons of fuel in six hours. How much fuel will you use each hour?

7. As you lift off, a flock of birds fly near the window. You count 138 birds by counting by twos. How many groups of two birds are there in the flock?

6. Take a look at those tiny houses as you ascend! There are six houses with white roofs, eight houses with black roofs, and nine houses with green roofs. How many houses do you see?

5. It's time to write a daily log. There are 64 pages and the rocket trip will last four days. How many pages must you write each day to complete the log?

4. Everyone is outside the school building waving to you. The students look like tiny bugs. You estimate the distance from the rocket to the school to be two miles. How many feet would that be? (5280 feet = 1 mile)

3. It's time for lunch. You drink eight ounces of water, eat four ounces of meat, six ounces of vegetables, and three ounces of dessert. How many ounces did you consume?

2. Everything becomes dark and stars appear in the distance. There are 28 stars in one group, 15 stars in one group, and 42 stars in one group. How many stars do you see?

1. The trip will last four days. How many hours will the trip last? How many minutes? How many seconds?

"The rocket trip is over. Check your answers with the answer key before you leave the rocket."

Just for Fun....

Make a picture dictionary of ten words from the rocket trip problems you have just solved.

snappy sets

Cover a shoe box with attractive wrapping paper. Place the following items inside the shoe box:

twenty bottle caps
fifty ice cream sticks
twenty-five paper clips
catalog
scissors
crayons
pencil
drawing paper
writing paper
paste
task materials and instructions

Print these directions on the inside top of the shoe box:

Follow the directions and complete the tasks.
Evaluate completed activities with the teacher.

Print these directions on an index card:

Use the bottle caps to show the sets of the following equations. Write each equation and the answer to each problem.

5 + 3 =	12 + 3 =
6 + 1 =	5 + 4 =
8 + 2 =	3 + 8 =
11 + 3 =	6 + 7 =
7 + 5 =	16 + 4 =
9 + 4 =	15 + 3 =

Print these directions on an index card:

Use the paper clips to show the
sets of ten addition and ten
subtraction problems. Write
each problem.

Example:

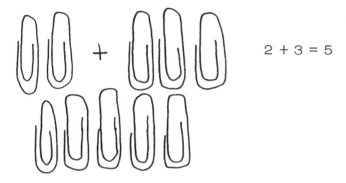

$2 + 3 = 5$

Print these directions on a piece of construction
paper:

Use the ice cream sticks to show the sets
of each of the following in the classroom.
Write an equation and answer for each
group of sets.

the boys and the girls
the windows and the doors
blondes and brunettes
students wearing blue and students
    wearing red
students wearing tennis shoes and
    students wearing regular shoes
desks and chairs

Cut a piece of poster board in the shape of
a catalog. Print these directions on the
catalog:

Look in the catalog and cut
out pictures to make sets.
Paste the pictures in sets
on the drawing paper.
Write an equation for each
group of sets.

Example:

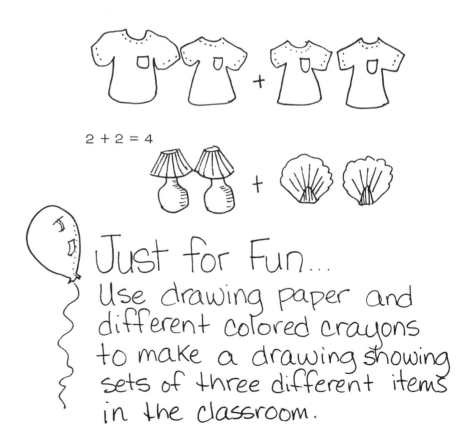

$2 + 2 = 4$

Just for Fun...
Use drawing paper and
different colored crayons
to make a drawing showing
sets of three different items
in the classroom.

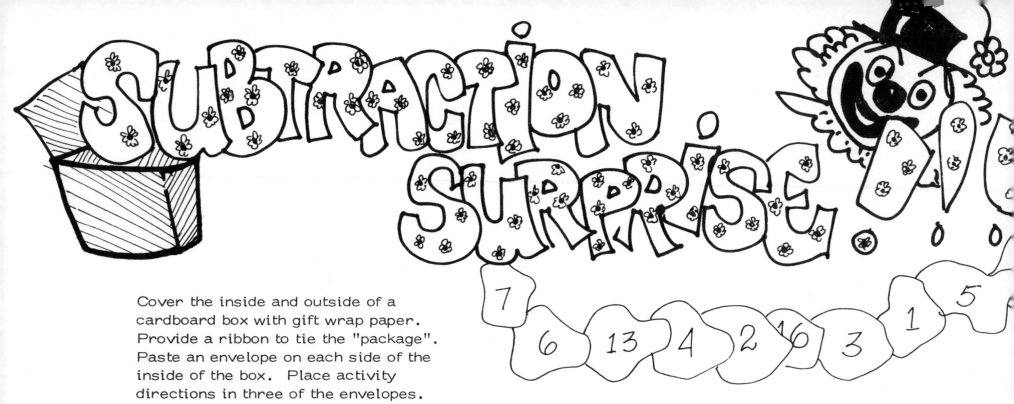

Subtraction Surprise

7 6 13 4 2 10 3 1 5

Cover the inside and outside of a cardboard box with gift wrap paper. Provide a ribbon to tie the "package". Paste an envelope on each side of the inside of the box. Place activity directions in three of the envelopes. Stash a surprise candy treat in the fourth envelope. Label the envelopes I, II, III, and IV. Place writing paper, drawing paper, pencil, and crayons in the bottom of the box.

Print these directions on an index card and glue to the inside of the box top:

> Follow the directions and complete each task. Evaluate completed activities with the teacher.

Cut fifty different shaped cards from tagboard. On each card write a number 0 – 20. Cut twenty-five different shaped cards and leave them blank. Print the directions on a 3 x 5" index card and place in Envelope I.

> Make a subtraction snake. Shuffle the numbered cards and place them face down. Draw two cards and place them on the floor to form a subtraction fact. Take a blank card and write the answer. Continue to draw cards and write the answer until all the cards have been used and the snake is complete. Draw and color a head for the snake.

106

Enlarge the maze and place it in
Envelope II.

Follow the maze by
solving each subtraction
problem.

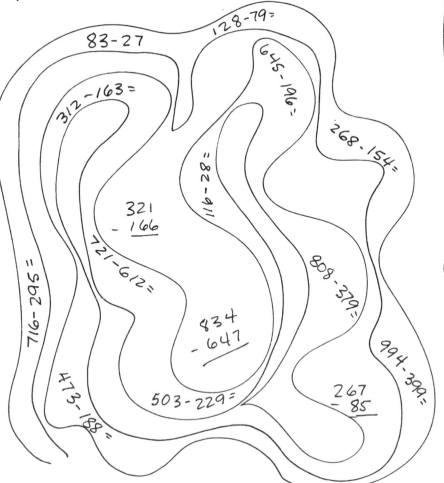

83-27

128-79=

312-163=

645-196=

268-154=

116-28=

321
- 166

721-612=

716-295=

834
- 647

808-379=

473-188=

503-229=

267
- 85

994-399=

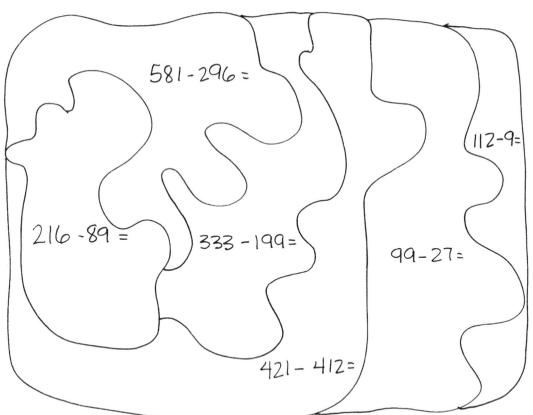

581-296=

112-9=

216-89=

333-199=

99-27=

421-412=

Paste a magazine picture on a piece of tagboard. Cut the
picture into puzzle pieces. Print a subtraction problem on
each puzzle piece. Print the following instructions on an
index card and place in Envelope III:

Select a puzzle piece and solve the subtraction
problem. Continue until the puzzle is complete.

Just for Fun...

Pretend you are on a safari.
Make a jungle of subtraction
problems and make your
way through the jungle.

THE BIG SWITCH

Place the following items in a large basket:

pint, quart, and liter containers
ruler showing inches and centimeters
centigrade and Fahrenheit thermometers
reference book on weights and measures
thermos bottle filled with hot tea
thermos bottle filled with ice water
scarf
belt
comb
writing paper
pencil
task instructions

Print these directions on an index card and place in the basket.

Follow the directions and complete each task. Evaluate completed activities with the teacher.

Make a large ruler using a piece of tagboard. Print the following directions on the ruler:

Use the ruler to measure the following items:

scarf	belt
comb	thermometer
reference book	writing paper
pencil	height of the pint, quart, and liter containers

Record the measurement of each item in inches and centimeters.

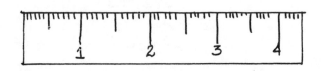

Print these directions on a piece of construction paper:

Use the centigrade and Fahrenheit thermometers to compare the temperatures of:

hot tea
ice water
hot and cold water from the faucet
outside temperature
classroom temperature
hall temperature

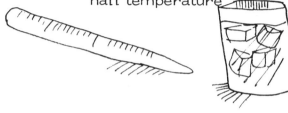

Cut a piece of poster board in the shape of a quart milk carton. Print these directions on the container:

Use the water at a sink and compare the measurements of the following:

pint – liter
quart – liter
half gallon – liters
gallon – liters

Just for Fun...

Measure ten items in the classroom. Record the measurements in inches and centimeters.

THE GOOD EGG

Directions . . . . .

Paint the outside of an egg carton with tempera paint. Secure twelve plastic eggs that can be opened. Place a story problem in eleven of the eggs. Place a candy treat in the twelfth egg. Place the twelve eggs, writing paper, drawing paper, crayons, and a pencil in the egg carton.

Print each story problem on a strip of paper, fold it, and place it in a plastic egg.

1. Farmer Jones wants to raise chickens so he can sell eggs. There are 48 nests. Two chickens can use the same nest. How many chickens does the farmer need? (2 points)

2. There are 96 chickens. If each chicken lays three eggs a day, how many eggs are there? (3 points)

3. The farmer gathers the eggs in baskets. There are six baskets and 378 eggs. How many eggs will be in each basket? (10 points)

4. The eggs are sold to the store in one-dozen egg cartons. There are 504 eggs. How many dozen will this be? (5 points)

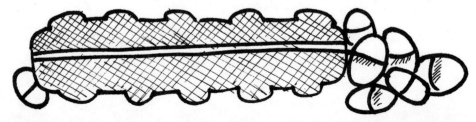

5. One dozen eggs cost 79¢. How much will three dozen eggs cost? (8 points)

6. A cake recipe calls for four eggs. If you triple the recipe, how many eggs will be needed to make the cake? (6 points)

7. A restaurant sells one egg, bacon, and toast for $1.45. How much would it cost a family of six to eat breakfast at the restaurant? (10 points)

8. An egg is cracked in half before cooking. If there are 36 shells, how many eggs have been cooked? (4 points)

9. The class is having an Easter egg hunt. There are 28 students and each student is to bring 6 eggs. How many eggs will there be? (7 points)

10. The egg section at the grocery store holds fifty dozen egg cartons. How many eggs are there in the egg section? (12 points)

11. Candy eggs are given as a treat in the classroom. There are 24 students and 120 eggs. How many candy eggs will each student receive? (9 points)

Print these directions on an index card. Paste the card on the inside lid of the egg carton.

Solve each story problem. Each correct answer is worth a certain number of points. Total your points and list them on the Good Egg Bulletin Board.

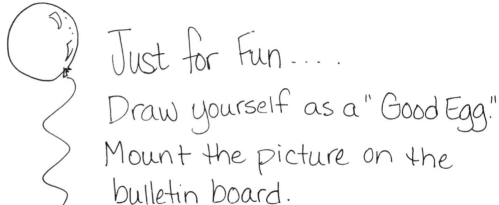

Just for Fun . . . .
Draw yourself as a "Good Egg."
Mount the picture on the bulletin board.

Tape the top of the shoe box to the bottom. Paint the box and draw a grandfather's clock on the top of the shoe box. Open one end of the box and place the following items in the box:

writing paper   drawing paper
pencil   crayons
task materials and instructions

Print these directions on the inside of the box top:

Follow the directions and complete each task. Evaluate completed activities with the teacher.

Cut twenty circles from tagboard and place them in an envelope. Print these directions on the envelope:

What is your favorite day of the week? What exciting things happen on this day? Show a schedule of your favorite day by drawing a clock face and the time of each activity on the circles. Write the name of the activity on the back of each clock.

Take two rectangular pieces of tagboard. Print
different times on one piece of tagboard. Draw
clock faces and show the same times that are
written on the other piece of tagboard. Punch
holes along the sides of the pieces of tagboard.
Attach pieces of yarn to one piece of tagboard.

Print these directions on the back of one
of the pieces of tagboard:

Lace the yarn to the correct
time on the clock.

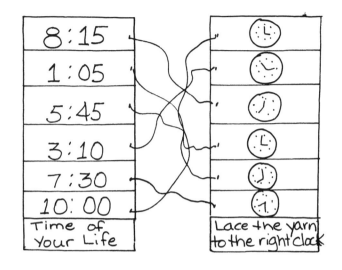

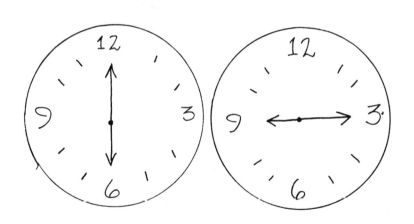

Cut fifteen circles from tagboard. Draw a
clock face on both sides of each circle.
Draw a different time on each clock. Place
the clocks in an envelope. Print task
directions on the envelope:

Look at each clock. Write the times
that are shown on both sides. Compare
the times and write how many minutes
and hours there are between the two
times.

Just for Fun.....
Create a digital clock you
would like to give to a
friend on a special occasion.
Show the time!

113

times tale

Cover a hose box with a bright color of fadeless paper. Design the top of the box to resemble a book jacket. Print Times Tale on the top of the box. Place the following items in the box.

spinner   pencil
writing paper   task instructions

Print these directions on the lid of the hose box:

Follow the directions and complete the tasks. Evaluate completed activities with the teacher.

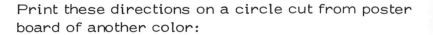

Make a spinner by cutting a circle from brightly colored poster board. Divide the circle into eight sections. Print these numbers in the sections: 2, 3, 4, 5, 6, 7, 8, 9. Fasten a paper clip with a metal brad in the center of the circle.

Print these directions on a circle cut from poster board of another color:

Flip the spinner and write the number on which the spinner stopped. Add a multiplication sign. (Example: 2 x) Flip the spinner again and write the number on which the spinner stopped. Write the answer to the equation. (Example: 2 x 9 = 18) Continue until you have twenty equations.

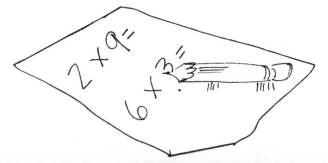

Print these directions on a piece of construction paper:

Write a story that includes numbers. Every time you write a number in the story write the multiplication fact that equals the number.

Example:

One day 6 (3 × 2) children went shopping. On the way to the store, they saw 16 (8 × 2) (4 × 4) signs.

Down:

1. (3 × 4) + 12 =
2. (6 × 8) + 5 =
3. (9 × 7) − 38 =
6. (3 × 24) − 36 =
7. (2 × 4) × 10 =
10. (5 × 15) + 25 − 18 =
11. (6 × 65) + 19 =
12. (2 × 87) − 26 =
17. (3 × 328) − 297 =
18. (9 × 3) × 3 =
21. (3 × 3) × (4 × 2) =
22. 4 × 19 =

Across:

1. 2 × 126 =
4. (4 × 120) − 45 =
5. (8 × 9) × 8 =
6. (6 × 18) + 193 =
7. 3 × 274 =
8. (9 × 5) + 9 =
9. (8 × 12) + 3 − 16 =
13. (2 × 3) × (2 × 4) =
14. (7 × 7) + 45 =
15. (3 × 267) + 99 =
16. (3 × 2) × (6 × 2) =
19. (4 × 4) × (3 × 2) =
20. 3 × 96 =

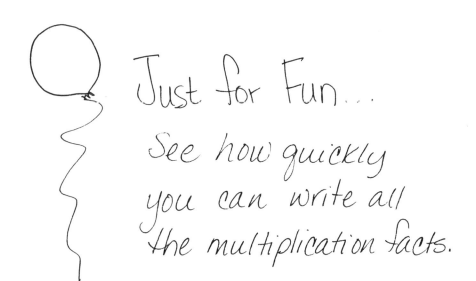

Just for Fun...
See how quickly you can write all the multiplication facts.

A Stitch in Time

Place the following items in a sewing basket:

small boy and girl dolls
samples of different fabrics
   (velvet, calico, denim, etc.)
scissors
tissue paper
tape measure
needle
thread
scraps of ribbon, lace, etc.
buttons
writing paper
pencils
watercolors
task instructions

Draw and cut out a shape to resemble a needle. Print these directions on the needle and tape to the lid of the sewing basket:

Follow the directions and complete each task. Evaluate completed activities with the teacher.

Draw and cut out a shape from tagboard to resemble a pair of scissors. Print these directions on the scissors:

You are a fashion designer for a large clothing company. Use the tape measure to find the doll's measurements. Make a pattern from tissue paper that includes the correct measurements to create a new outfit for the doll.

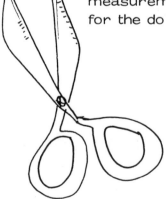

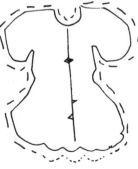

Draw and cut out a shape from tagboard to resemble a spool of thread. Print these directions on the thread:

Select a piece of fabric. Place the doll's outfit pattern on the fabric and cut it out. Use needle, thread, lace, ribbon, and buttons to complete the outfit. Let the doll model the new clothes!

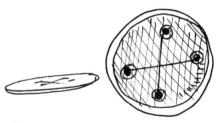

Draw and cut out a shape to resemble a button. Print these directions on the button:

Examine each piece of fabric. Write three descriptive words for each piece of fabric. (Example: velvet – red, soft, fuzzy) Examine the piece of fabric again and try to write three words that are more colorful and exciting. (Example: velvet – crimson, elegant, crinkly)

Draw and cut out a shape from tagboard to resemble a thimble. Print these directions on the thimble:

Use writing paper to record an identity for the doll. Give the following vital statistics:

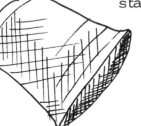

Name: _____

Full Address _____

_____

Sex _____ Age _____

Occupation and Job

Description _____

_____

Hobbies _____

_____

Just for Fun...

Plan an exciting vacation to suit the life role you gave the doll. Design a vacation wardrobe, luggage, and any special equipment needed for the vacation.

Blue Plate Special

Arrange a stack of five paper plates. Number the plates one through five. Make masking tape loops on plate number one to hold a pencil and blue and green crayons. Print task instructions as specified in each activity on the plates. Arrange the plates numerically with number one on top of the stack and number five on the bottom. Tie the stack together with blue yarn or crepe paper strips.

Print these directions on plate number one:

Follow the directions and complete each task. Evaluate completed activities with the teacher.

Paper clip a sheet of drawing paper to plate number two. Print these directions on the plate:

If you could own and operate a very successful restaurant what would you want it to be like? Here's your chance to plan a "dream restaurant". Will it be Italian, Chinese, Mexican, a Steak House, or Hamburger Heaven? Give your restaurant a name and use the crayons to picture it on the sheet of drawing paper attached to this plate.

Fold a sheet of drawing paper in half and tape to plate number three. Print these directions on the plate:

> Create a special menu for your restaurant. The funny thing about your menu is that all the appetizers have names beginning with M, all the salads with C, the meats with S, the vegetables with T, and the desserts with B. Use your imagination to make the food interesting and design the cover of the menu to add real excitement to the dining experience.

Paper clip a sheet of writing paper to plate number four. Print these directions on the plate:

> Now that you know exactly what kind of restaurant you will have you need to find your staff. Write role descriptions for all the people you will need to help you operate the restaurant. Use the back of the sheet of writing paper to write a newspaper ad to fill the positions.

Paper clip a sheet of writing paper to plate number five. Print these directions on the plate:

Plan a budget for your restaurant. Try to balance the income with the expenditures.

Menu

◇ Marvelous
        Mushrooms
Crispy
        Cucumbers
Sizzling
        Steak
◇ Tasty Turnips
Beautiful
        Blueberries

Tomatoes ¢ Lettuce
$ $ ¢ $ ¢
Bananas   Steak
$
Baked Potatoes

Just for Fun...
Stage a "grand opening" celebration for your restaurant. Plan the invitations, special food, favors and entertainment.

CONTROL CENTER

Secure a round
ice cream container
from an ice cream shop.
Cover the ice cream
container with contact
paper. Cut five circles from tagboard and
paint them different colors. Print the task
directions on the circles and paste them on
the outside of the ice cream container. Place
the following items in the container:

writing paper
drawing paper
pencil
crayons
study guide

Print these directions on a tagboard circle:

Follow the directions and complete
each task. Evaluate completed
activities with the teacher.

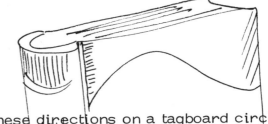

Print these directions on a tagboard circle:

You are the owner of a book store.
A customer comes in your store
wanting to buy a book on self-discipline.
Draw and design the book jacket that is
on the book which you will show the
customer. Give the book a title and
show an example of self-discipline
on the book jacket.

Print these directions on a tagboard circle:

Use one of the following ideas and write a story that reflects self-discipline:

do your homework	or	watch television
eat dessert	or	lose weight
play games	or	do your chores
practice piano	or	take a nap

Print these directions on a tagboard circle:

Read the study guide and write a report on self-discipline. Plan a class panel discussion on self-discipline. Write six questions you will submit.

Print these directions on a tagboard circle:

You receive an allowance of $10 each month. You are tempted to spend the allowance for one item or spend the money the first day and not have any money left for the rest of the month. Use self-discipline and plan a budget showing how you will spend your allowance.

Just for Fun...
Design a "good self-control" badge. Present the badge to a deserving friend.

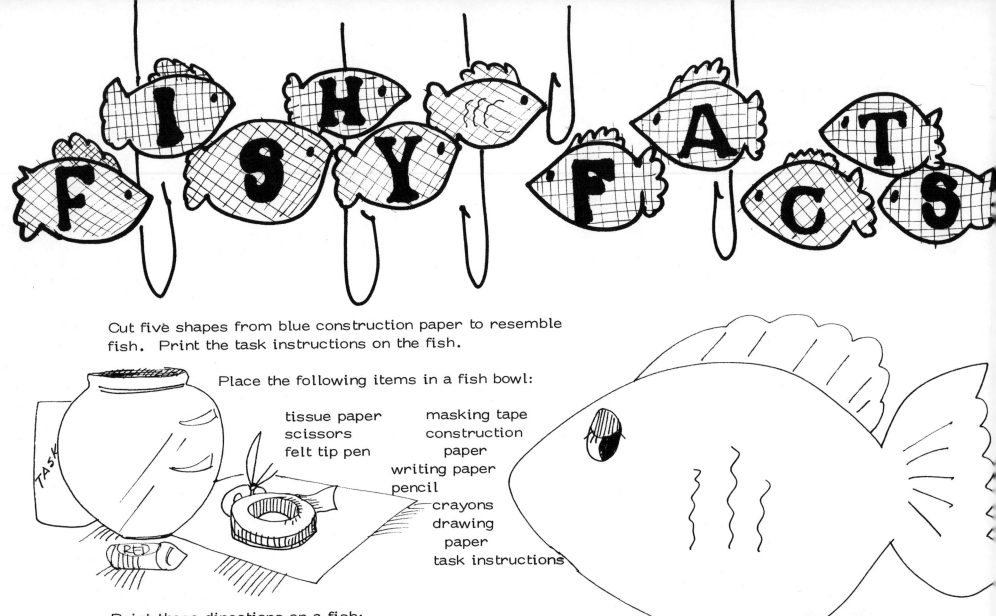

Cut five shapes from blue construction paper to resemble fish. Print the task instructions on the fish.

Place the following items in a fish bowl:

tissue paper masking tape
scissors construction
felt tip pen paper
writing paper
pencil
crayons
drawing
paper
task instructions

Print these directions on a fish:

Follow the directions and complete each task. Evaluate completed activities with the teacher.

Print these directions on a fish:

Remove all the items from the fish bowl and use tissue paper and construction paper to create an underwater scene in the fish bowl. Tape the objects to the fish bowl so they can be removed easily.

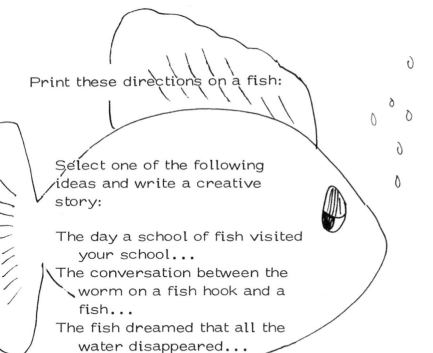

Print these directions on a fish:

Select one of the following ideas and write a creative story:

The day a school of fish visited your school...

The conversation between the worm on a fish hook and a fish...

The fish dreamed that all the water disappeared...

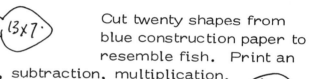

Cut twenty shapes from blue construction paper to resemble fish. Print an addition, subtraction, multiplication, or division problem on each fish. Print these directions on a larger fish and place all the fish in a plastic bag:

See what a good fisherman you are! Catch a fish by solving the math problem on a piece of writing paper. You receive two points for each fish you catch. Total your points and record the score at the bottom of the paper.

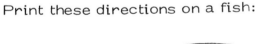

Print these directions on a fish:

Make a list of the different ways fish can be eaten. Show a pictorial report tracing a fish from the sea to the table.

Just for Fun...
Write a fisherman's tale.

HABIT FORMING

Place the following on a tray:

writing paper   crayons
drawing paper   two paper bags
pencil   tempera paint
task instructions

Print these directions on an index card and tape on the tray:

Follow the directions and complete each task. Evaluate completed activities with the teacher.

Print these directions on an index card:

This week has been designated as "Good Study Habits Week". A prize will be given for the best "Good Study Habits Week" poster. Enter your poster in the contest!

Print these directions on an index card:

Write a script for a puppet show involving two characters. Use good study habits as the theme. The puppets can be animals or people.

Print these directions on an index card:

Make a list of ten good study habits and a list of five poor study habits. Write a paragraph telling how you can improve your study habits.

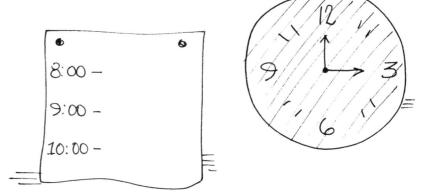

Print these directions on an index card:

Make a time schedule showing how you currently budget your time for schoolwork. Develop a plan to use your time wisely for one week.

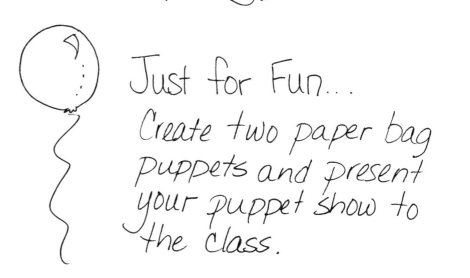

Just for Fun... Create two paper bag puppets and present your puppet show to the class.

HEART BREAKERS

Cut four large hearts from red
construction paper.

Place the following items in a heart-
shaped candy box:

writing paper

drawing paper
red construction paper
paste
pencil
task instructions

GLUE

Print these directions on the lid of the candy box:

Follow the directions and complete each
task. Evaluate completed activities with
the teacher.

Print these directions on a heart:

Tear red construction paper
into tiny pieces. Use a piece
of drawing paper and the tiny
pieces of red construction
paper and create a heart mosaic.

Print these directions on a heart:

Develop a story using one of
the following story endings:

...the heart broke into pieces.
...was my heart beating.
...the heart disappeared.
...the heart was magic.
...the mysterious heartbeat.

Print these directions on a heart:

Cut a large heart from drawing
paper. Write the information
you know about your heart on
one side of the heart. Write
questions you would like to know
about your heart on the other
side of the heart.

Cut fifteen hearts. Cut each heart into different
fractional parts. Place the fractional hearts in a
plastic bag. Print these directions
on a heart and place inside the
plastic bag:

$\frac{1}{2}$

Match the
pieces to
form hearts.
Each heart
contains certain
fractional parts. Write
the fraction in each heart.

$\frac{1}{3}$

$\frac{1}{4}$

Just for Fun..
Write three clues about
yourself on a heart. Hide
the heart in a classmate's
desk. See how quickly you
are identified.

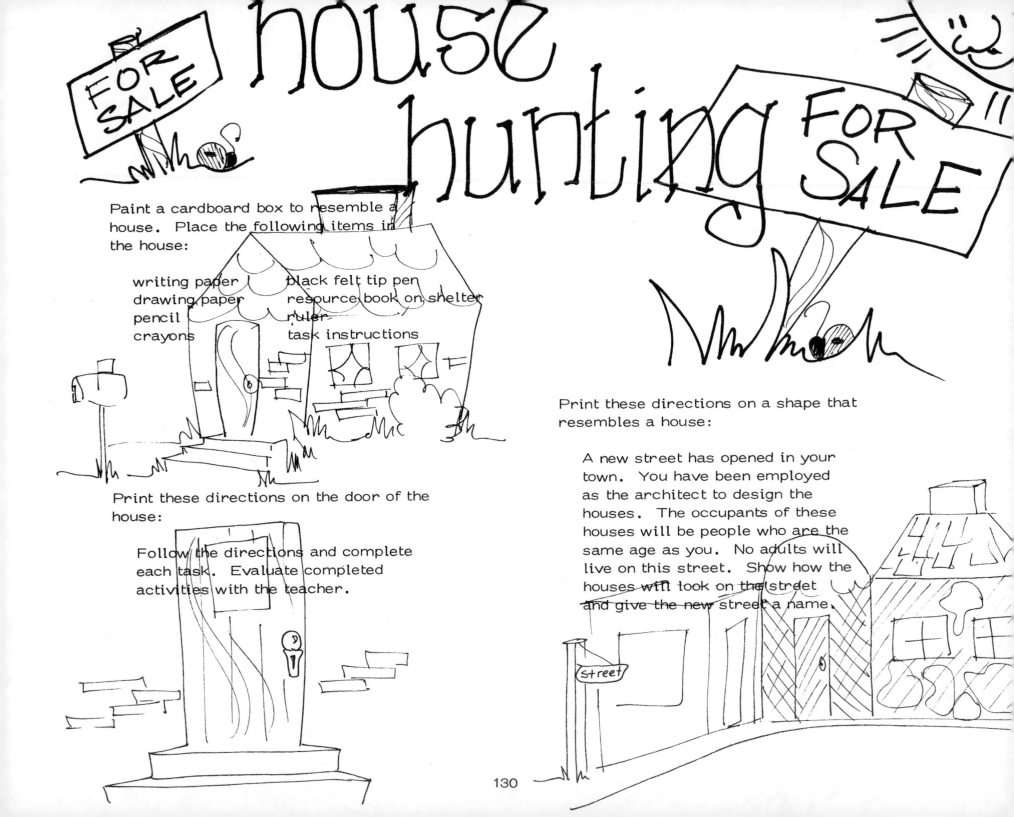

house hunting

FOR SALE

FOR SALE

Paint a cardboard box to resemble a house. Place the following items in the house:

writing paper
drawing paper
pencil
crayons

black felt tip pen
resource book on shelter
ruler
task instructions

Print these directions on the door of the house:

Follow the directions and complete each task. Evaluate completed activities with the teacher.

Print these directions on a shape that resembles a house:

A new street has opened in your town. You have been employed as the architect to design the houses. The occupants of these houses will be people who are the same age as you. No adults will live on this street. Show how the houses will look on the street and give the new street a name.

street

130

Make a For Sale sign. Print these directions on the sign:

You are a real estate agent and you have three houses for sale. Write an ad for each house to place in the daily newspaper.

Draw and cut out a shape to resemble an igloo. Print these directions on the igloo:

Use the resource book to locate information about different types of shelter. Write a short report on the various kinds of homes.

Draw and cut out a shape to resemble a ruler. Print these directions on the ruler:

Use the ruler to plan and design the inside of a house. List the outside measurements of the house and the measurements of each room in inches and centimeters. Add furniture to the rooms. Give the dimensions for each piece of furniture in inches and centimeters.

Just for Fun...

Draw your house. Cut the drawing into a jigsaw puzzle and ask a friend to work the puzzle.

Library Logo

Make a booklet by stapling five pieces of drawing paper together. Print the task instructions in the booklet.

Place the following items in a book satchel:

Print these directions in the booklet:

Go quietly to the library, follow the directions, and complete each task. Evaluate completed activities with the teacher.

study guide
shoe box
several library books
construction paper
tagboard
crayons
paste
shelf paper
writing paper
pencil
task instructions

Print these directions in the booklet:

The library is having a peep box display and you are invited to share your peep box. Use the shoe box, construction paper, tagboard, and crayons to create your entry illustrating a favorite library book.

Print these directions in the booklet:

Select a book from the library. Read the book and write a review. Mount the book review on the library bulletin board to entice your classmates to read the book.

Print these directions in the booklet:

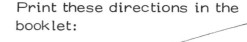

Select two books from each category of the Dewey Decimal System. Supply the following information for each category:

1. List the titles of the books.
2. Write a math problem to compare the length of the books.
3. Write a math problem to compare the number of chapters in the books.
4. Write math problems to compare the length of the chapters in each book.
5. Write a math problem to compare the copyright dates of the books.

Print these directions in the booklet:

Use shelf paper and draw pictures to create a filmstrip explaining the Dewey Decimal System. Write a script to accompany the filmstrip.

Just for Fun...
Plan a book club or contest to encourage students to read more library books.

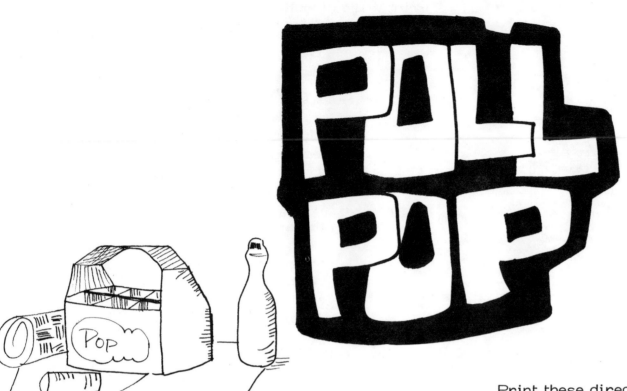

POLL POP

Place the following items in a six-bottle soda pop carton:

daily newspaper
drawing paper
writing paper
pencil
colored chalk
crayons
task instructions

Cut five shapes from colored poster board to resemble pop bottles. Print the task instructions on the pop bottles.

Print these directions on a pop bottle:

Follow the directions and complete each task. Evaluate completed activities with the teacher.

Print these directions on a pop bottle:

You have just completed a survey on art. The results are surprising because eighty percent of the people surveyed preferred the same type of art. Show an example of the art that eighty percent of the people selected.

Print these directions on a pop bottle:

Design a questionnaire to find out
the opinions of your classmates on
the following items:

1. Favorite animal
2. Favorite television program
3. Favorite snack food
4. Favorite sport
5. Favorite color

Add five other items to the questionnaire.
Distribute the questionnaire and ask
your classmates to return it to you.
Tabulate the results of your poll.

Print these directions on a pop bottle:

Take a newspaper survey. Use the
newspaper to locate and record the
following information:

1. Number of movies advertised
2. Number of restaurants advertised
3. Number of department stores advertised
4. Number of grocery stores advertised
5. Number of furniture stores advertised
6. Number of drug stores or variety stores
    advertised

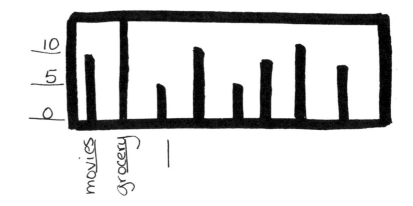

Print these directions on a pop bottle:

Use the information you collected
from the newspaper and make a
bar graph showing the results of
the survey. Drawing paper and
crayons can be used to make the
graph.

Just for Fun...
Ask three friends to
predict the weather for
the next three days.
Compare the predictions.

Place the following items in a cereal box:

    sample of cereal in a plastic bag
    shelf paper
    glue
    felt tip pens
    crayons
    pencil
    task instructions

Print these directions on a piece of colored construction paper:

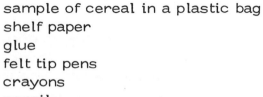

Print these directions on a piece of colored construction paper:

    Follow the directions and complete each task. Evaluate completed activities with the teacher.

Power Puffs is the name of a new cereal that has just been developed. A design is needed for the box. Empty the contents from the cereal box. Cover the box with shelf paper. Write the name of the new cereal and design one side of the cereal box.

Print these directions on a piece of colored construction paper:

Design one side of the box by writing descriptive words or phrases about the cereal and drawing pictures showing what the cereal will do for people who eat it.

Print these directions on a piece of colored construction paper:

Use one end of the cereal box and write the cereal ingredients. Write a paragraph telling why Power Puffs are nutritious.

Print these directions on a piece of colored construction paper:

Write the recipe for Power Puffs on one end of the cereal box. Write the weight of the cereal in ounces and grams. Don't forget to stamp the price on the box of cereal!

Just for Fun...
Enjoy the sample of Power Puffs.

Place the following items in a brown paper bag:

book about rocks
tempera paint
8 x 11" poster board
glue
pencil
writing paper
task instructions

Print these directions on a piece of colored construction paper:

Follow the directions and complete each task. Evaluate completed activities with the teacher.

Print these directions on a piece of colored construction paper:

Take a thirty-minute walking field trip around the school grounds. Find as many different rocks as you can. Use the resource book and try to identify each rock. Use glue and mount the rocks on a piece of poster board. Label each rock.

Print these directions on a piece of colored construction paper:

Use one of the rocks that you found on the field trip to make a "rock critter". Use tempera paint to give your rock critter personality.

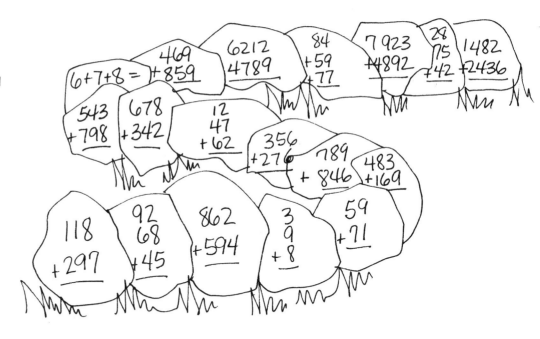

Print these directions on a piece of colored construction paper:

You are the director of a museum. Write a letter to the school inviting the students to see the rock exhibit. Include all the necessary information that would make the students excited about visiting the museum.

Enlarge the above game board. Print these directions on the back of the game board:

Complete the rock wall by solving each math problem.

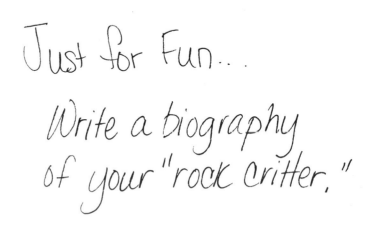

Just for Fun...

Write a biography of your "rock critter."

sandy signatures

Draw and cut out five shapes to
resemble sea shells.

Place the following items in a sand
bucket:

shovel
jar of sand
glue
drawing paper
writing paper
pencil
pastel chalk
task instructions

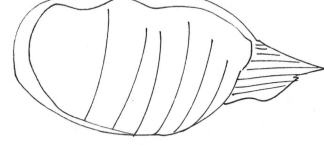

Print these directions on a paper shell
and tape it to the sand bucket:

Follow these directions and complete
each task. Evaluate completed
activities with the teacher.

Print these directions on a paper shell:

Outline an interesting beach scene
on a piece of drawing paper. Use
real sand and glue to fill in the
beach area. Finish the rest of the
scene with pastel chalk. Sign your
creation with your "real you"
signature.

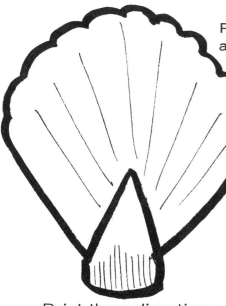

Print these directions on
a paper shell:

Place the shovel in the center of a
piece of drawing paper and trace
around the shovel. Fill the shovel
with as many words as you can make
from the letters in your first name.
Fill the space around the shovel
with words made from your last name.

Print these directions on a paper shell:

Pour the sand carefully on a sheet of drawing
paper. Use the eraser end of the pencil to
write your full name as you ordinarily write it.
Look at your name to see which letters need
improvement and how you can
make your signature more
artistically attractive. Erase
your signature and
practice "sand
writing" it until it
reflects the real
"you".

Print these
directions on a paper shell:

Pour the sand carefully on a sheet of drawing
paper. Use the eraser end of the pencil and
write an addition, subtraction, multiplication,
or division problem. Solve the problem in the
sand. Continue until you have
written twenty sand problems and
solved them.

Just for Fun...

Write a story about
the biggest and best sand
castle ever built.

Scissors Tale

Cut a scissors outline and letters to spell "Scissors Tale" from black construction paper. Stitch them on a canvas tote bag. Place the following items in the tote bag:

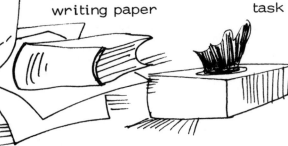

catalog	index cards
drawing paper	crayons
paste	tissue paper
pencil	scissors
writing paper	task instructions

Print these directions on an index card and stitch on the outside of the bag:

Follow the instructions to complete the tasks. Evaluate completed activities with the teacher.

Print these directions on an index card:

Lay the scissors flat on a piece of drawing paper and trace around them. Move and trace the scissors in different positions, overlapping, touching, linking, or as many other ways as you can to form an interesting design on the entire sheet of drawing paper. Use multi-color crayons to fill in spaces between lines. Complete the design by tracing around the lines with a black felt tip pen. Take your "Scissors Tale" design home to share with your family.

Print these directions on an index card:

Cut five circles, four triangles, three squares, and seven rectangles from colored tissue paper. Paste the shapes on five index cards. Make up one math problem for each set of shapes. Write additional problems on the cards. Give each card to a classmate to solve the problems on the back of the card. Have the cards returned to you for checking the correct answers.

Print these directions on an index card:

We sometimes tend to take tools such as scissors for granted. Make a list of at least ten purposes scissors are used for in your everyday life. Now try to substitute a means of accomplishing each of the tasks if you lived in a "scissorless" world.

Print these directions on an index card:

Cut pictures of four people and six articles the people might use from the catalog. Arrange the people and articles on a piece of drawing paper in a setting in which they might be participants. (Example: a family watching television, teenagers on a picnic, children playing ball, etc.) Write a suspense story with a surprise ending that the scene could be used to illustrate. When the story is completed, paste the pictures in place and display the illustrated story on the bulletin board.

Just for Fun...
Fold a piece of tissue paper in eight equal sections. Draw a doll figure, being careful not to cut through the edges of the fold. Cut out your string of paper dolls.

SHIP SHAPE

Paint a rectangular shaped facial tissue box to be used as a boat.

Cut a triangle from blue construction paper. Glue a plastic drinking straw to the triangle. Attach the straw to the tissue box to form a sailboat. Cut construction paper letters and paste them on the sail to form the title, Ship Shape. Place the following items in the sailboat:

writing paper   crayons
drawing paper   ruler
protractor   compass
kitchen plastic wrap   drinking straws
tissue paper   glue
          task instructions

Print these directions on the side of the sailboat:

Follow the directions and complete each task. Evaluate completed activities with the teacher.

Draw and cut out a shape to resemble an oar from tagboard. Print these directions

on

the

oar:

Glue four drinking straws in the shape of a square. Cover the square with clear plastic kitchen wrap. Cut different shapes from colored tissue paper. Make a collage by pasting the tissue paper shapes on the clear plastic. Attach a piece of yarn to the top of the collage and hang your stained glass window.

144

Draw and cut out a tagboard oar. Print these directions on the oar:

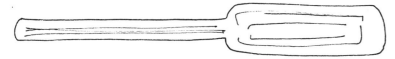

You are the passenger in a spaceship which has just landed on a strange planet covered with many different shapes. The shapes cover the window of the spaceship and you can no longer see out. Your only clue as to life on the planet is the voices you hear. Surprisingly enough, you can under-stand the language. Listen carefully and write the dialogue that is taking place outside the spaceship. Be sure to use quotation marks where they are needed.

Draw and cut out a tagboard oar. Print these directions on the oar:

Take a nature walk around the school grounds. Collect living and non-living items. Look at each item and list the different shapes that are observable in each object. Example: tree branch – cylinder

acorn – circle

Draw and cut out a tagboard oar. Print these directions on the oar:

Use the protractor, compass, or ruler and draw and label an example of each of the following:

circle   isosceles triangle
quadrangle   parallelogram
trapezoid   square
right angle   rectangle
hexagon   pentagon

Just for Fun....

Take a picture of some of the unusual shapes on the strange Planet. to show your friends on earth!

Sports SPECIAL

Place the following items in a football helmet:

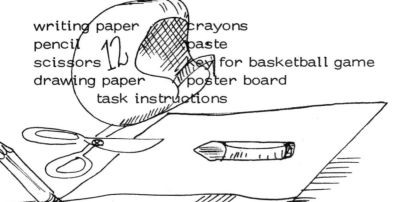

    writing paper   crayons
    pencil   paste
    scissors   key for basketball game
    drawing paper   poster board
       task instructions

Draw and cut out a shape to resemble a baseball bat. Print these directions on the baseball bat:

    Draw, color, and cut out five pictures
    showing five people participating in
    different sports. Paste the pictures on
    a piece of poster board to make a collage.
    Give your collage a title.

Draw and cut out a shape to resemble a football. Print these directions on the football and tape them on the helmet:

    Follow the directions and complete
    each task. Evaluate completed
    activities with the teacher.

Draw and cut out a shape to resemble a tennis racquet. Print these directions on the tennis racquet:

Write a creative story based on one of the following ideas:

The basketball disappears and...
The chessmen decide to...
The race car runs out of gas and...
The hockey puck is cold and...
The boxer loses the boxing gloves and...

Enlarge the basketball game board. Draw and cut out a shape to resemble a basketball. Print these directions on the basketball:

See how many points you can score in the basketball game by solving each problem on the basketball court. You receive two points for each correct problem. Total your points.

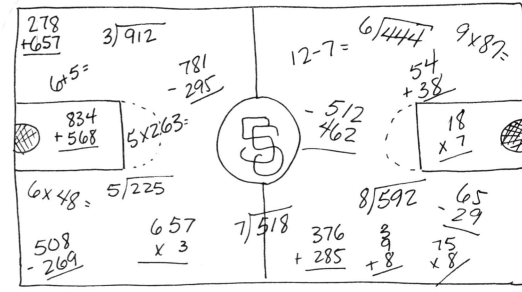

Draw and cut out a shape to resemble a hockey stick. Print these directions on the hockey stick:

You are the coach of a competitive sport. Make a list of suggestions to help the team become more physically fit. Include the following items: food, rest, and exercise.

Just for Fun...
Design a uniform for your favorite sport.

STOP, LOOK, and LISTEN

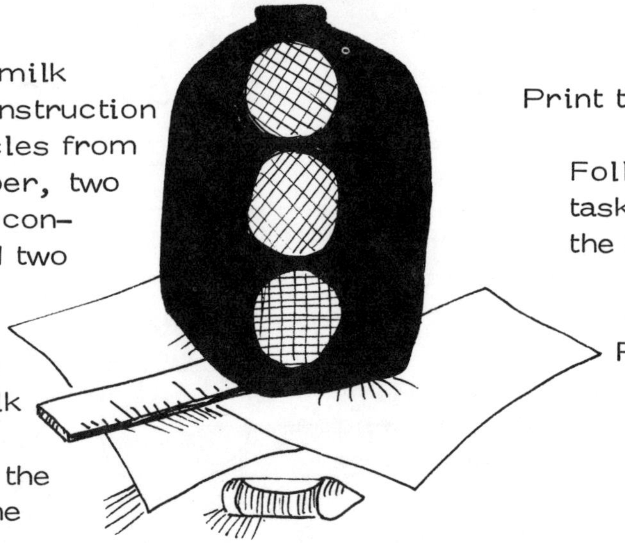

Cover a half-gallon milk carton with black construction paper. Cut two circles from red construction paper, two circles from yellow construction paper, and two circles from green construction paper. Paste the circles on both sides of the milk carton to create a traffic light. Place the following items in the traffic light:

drawing paper crayons
writing paper ruler
pencil task instructions

Print these directions on a yellow caution light:

Follow the directions and complete each task. Evaluate completed activities with the teacher.

Print these directions on a red light:

Design a surprise sign for the classroom. The message on the sign has never been used before. Hang the sign in a special place in the classroom.

Print these directions on a green light:

You have just arrived in strange and exciting Signville. All the signs are different, seem mixed up, and can even talk. Write a creative story telling about your adventure in Signville.

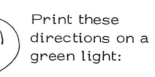

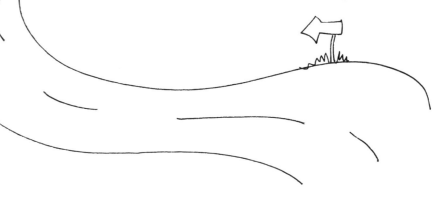

Print these directions on a green light:

Draw a bicycle trail map of your neighborhood. Include signs on the trail. Use a ruler to draw the map. Provide a legend in inches and centimeters for the map.

Print these directions on a red light:

Make a list of the different signs that are used by and are important to our society. Write a sentence or sentences explaining how the signs are helpful or necessary.

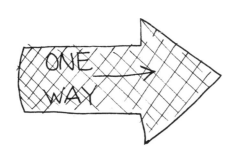

Just for Fun.
Take a walking field trip in the school building. Make a note of all the signs that you see.

Suitcase Skills

Draw and cut out five shapes to resemble travel stickers. Print the task instructions on the stickers and tape them to the suitcase.

Place the following items in a suitcase:

encyclopedia A and P
encyclopedia that includes your state
drawing paper
crayons
string
paste
scissors
coat hanger
writing paper
pencil
task instructions

Print these directions on a travel sticker:

Read the information on airplanes in the encyclopedia. Draw and color five pictures of different airplanes. Cut out the airplanes and attach them to a wire coat hanger to make an airplane mobile.

Print these directions on a travel sticker:

Follow the directions and complete each task. Evaluate completed activities with the teacher.

Print these directions on a travel sticker:

You have been employed to travel and promote your state in hopes that more people will want to visit, build factories, or move to your state. Use the encyclopedia and learn more about your state. Make a brochure that includes pictures and information about your state.

VISIT Our Town

Print these directions on a travel sticker:

Use the encyclopedia and find the following information about each planet.

1. average distance from the sun
2. length of orbit
3. diameter

Use the information and write a math problem comparing the earth with each planet.

(Example: Diameter – Earth – 7,927 miles

Mars – 4,200 miles

$$\frac{}{3,727}$$

Print these directions on a travel sticker:

A zoo is being planned for your city and you are on the committee to secure the animals. Use the encyclopedia and read about animals. Make an outline and write a report on animals to present to the zoo committee.

Popcorn

Admit One

Just for Fun...
Spend extra time finding other information in the encyclopedia.

Place the following items in a
shoe bag:

junk art supplies
map of your country
calendar
paste
writing paper
pencil

What? What is it?

Use the junk art supplies and create
a piece of art. Give your creation
a title and display it in the classroom.

Print the above directions on an index card.

Print these directions on an index card:

Follow the directions and
complete each task. Evaluate
completed activities with the
teacher.

Print these directions on an index card:

Who? Who are you?

Write your biography.
Do not sign your name.
Mount the biography on the
bulletin board and let your classmates guess the identity of the
biographer.

Me

Print these directions on an index card:

When? When do these events occur?

Use the calendar and write the day of the
week, day of the month, and the month to the
following:

1. Your birthday
2. Next holiday
3. Last holiday
4. Two weeks from today
5. Six weeks ago

6. The next time your favorite television
   program will be shown
7. Yesterday
8. First day of school
9. Last day of school
10. Day before yesterday

Print these directions on an index card:

Where? Where are these
places?

Use the map to locate the following
places:

1. The capital of your country.
2. The capital of your home state.
3. The largest state of your country.
4. The smallest state of your country.
5. A national park you would like to
   visit
6. The largest city in your country.

Just for Fun...
Write four questions that
can be answered by who,
what, when, and where. Let
a friend answer the questions.

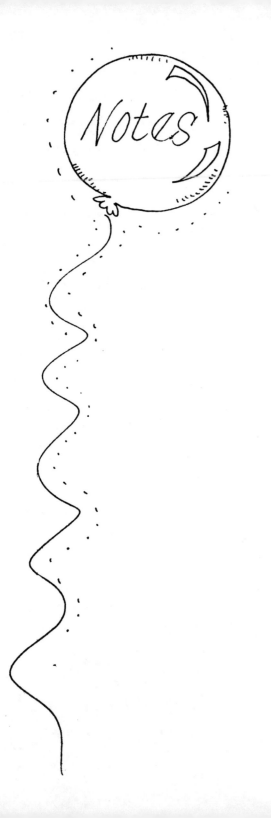

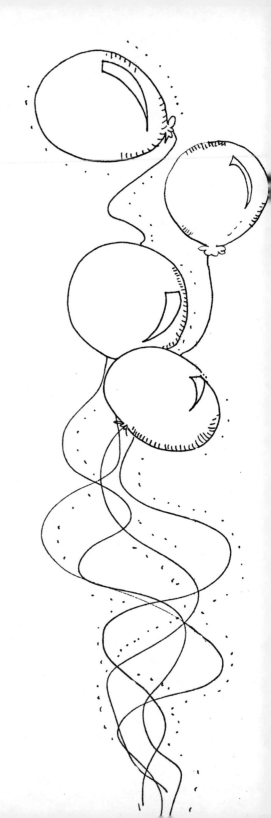

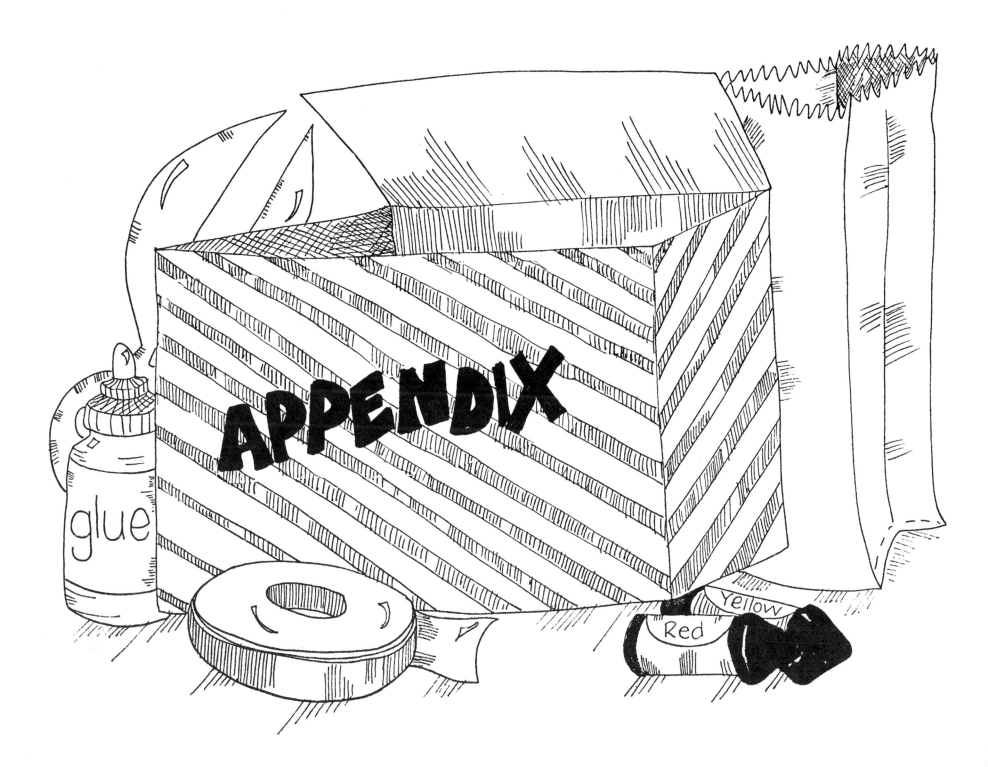

Teachers need to have some fun too! The mini-centers presented in this book were designed to add a bit of sparkle to life in the classroom. The following suggestions are added to encourage teachers to stop to look about, to perhaps think about a thing or two in their ordinary everyday environment in a new or different way, and to seek their own "just for fun" approach to teaching and learning.

Stage a classroom circus or carnival. Invite another class to be guests and be sure to provide popcorn and balloons for everybody.

Ask each student to select, copy, and illustrate a beautiful poem or a meaningful quotation to be mounted on a specially prepared classroom bulletin board.

Keep anecdotal record cards and use a good socio-gram to help you to know more about your students.

Invite a fellow teacher to join you on an excursion to the Goodwill or Salvation Army store to look for "good junk" to recycle via the elementary classroom. Game boards, outdated text and workbooks, baskets, boxes of all kinds, posters, bean bag chairs, throw rugs, and dress-up clothes are some "jewels" seen in one creative teacher's collection.

Make or buy a mailbox for your classroom. Station it in a convenient place and solicit "feedback" from your students. Urge them to be candid in sharing thoughts and feelings about practices and procedures and about the emotional and intellectual climate of the classroom.

Christen the mailbox idea by writing a note to every student. Think hard to find one very special thing to say to each student that will show your awareness of that student as a unique human being worthy of personal dignity and respect.

Skip a planned directed teaching session and enjoy an impromptu music, story, or art session with your students. Enjoy is the key word. Forget teaching and learning for this short period—just relax and share the good warm feeling that is sure to abound.

Develop your own "merit badge" to pin on deserving students at appropriate times.

Devise a unique graffiti system to convey good will and take some of the drudgery out of paper grading or center checking. It could be a smiling face, sunshine symbol, gold star, a stylized okay, or maybe something much more creative and original. The only important factor is its communicative meaning to you and your students.

Initiate the idea and assist your students in planning an open house for their parents. Nothing fancy-- just a time set aside to say "come to school to see what we do and how we do it". Try to adjust the time and space expectations for as many parents as possible.

Invite your students to rearrange furniture and equipment to create their ideal classroom. This may result in chaos, and the finished (or unfinished) project may be totally unworkable, but the decision-making should cause some lively group dynamics and healthy interaction. Also the follow-up discussion is sure to be highly enlightening.

Set aside a Saturday to tour garage sales and/or the local flea market. As a special bonus to yourself, add the farmer's market to the itinerary.

Secure a good collection of outdated travel brochures from a travel agent. Present them with encyclopedias, road maps, atlases, travel magazines, and posters and ask your students to plan the trip they'd most like to take. Plan your own trip at the same time. Who knows, dreams do sometimes come true!

Take a field trip to a local school supply store. Treat yourself to two "ready-to-use" games or activity packages to make learning in your classroom more fun. Remember, teacher time is valuable and you don't want to spend all your time making instructional materials--even though your students do like your original ones best of all.

Ask each student in your group to contribute one container to be used as the inspiration for a mini-center. On "mini-center idea day" the containers and the center ideas for their use may be presented to the group.

Assemble as many containers as students in the group and ask each student to select one container in which center activities can be developed.

Set aside twenty (or maybe even thirty) minutes of every school day for every person in the room (including teachers and visitors) to read a book.

Beg, borrow, or steal a rocking chair for your classroom.

Substitute a good old fashioned "spell-down" for the weekly spelling test every once in a while.

Read The Geranium On The Window Sill Just Died, But Teacher You Went Right On, Albert Cullum, Harlin Quist.

Go to a local ice cream parlor to secure empty ice cream cartons to use for mini center containers. Since you're there anyway, treat yourself to a hot fudge sundae. You deserve it!

Treasures for Mini-Center Creators

cereal and detergent boxes

old game boards

cardboard tubes

wallpaper and wallpaper books

greeting cards

small tools

beans and beads

paper plates and cups

dress-up clothes

recipes

puzzles..jigsaw, crossword, and brain teasers

baskets

hats

maps

scraps of lumber, felt, burlap, or vinyl

coffee cans

plastic containers

potato chip cans

plastic eggs..hosiery containers or Easter novelties

tennis ball cans

milk cartons

shopping bags

box tops and can tops

straws

catalogs

newspapers

tin cans..all sizes

old photographs

jars

pipe cleaners

old suitcases

wood scraps

sectioned boxes..liquor store a good source

window shades

pizza boards and boxes

pillows

styrofoam

scrapbooks and photo albums

egg cartons

wooden dowels

plastic bleach bottles

foam rubber scraps

record covers

curtain rods

travel posters

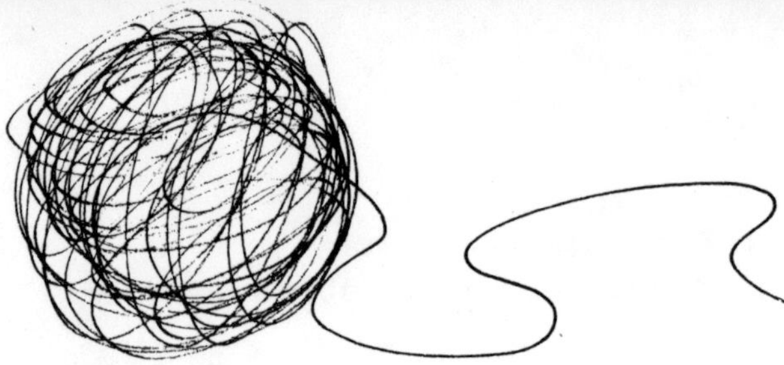

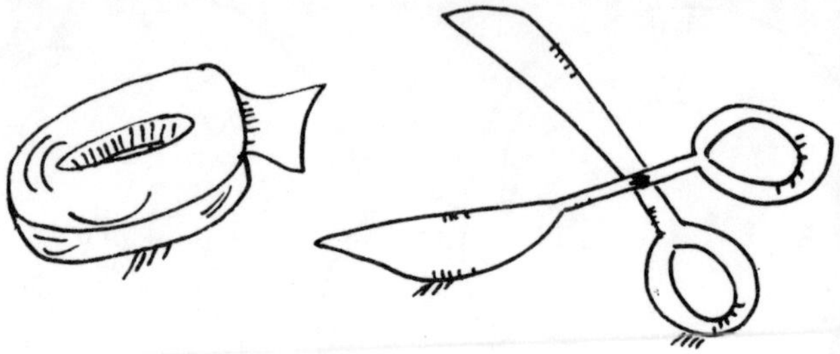

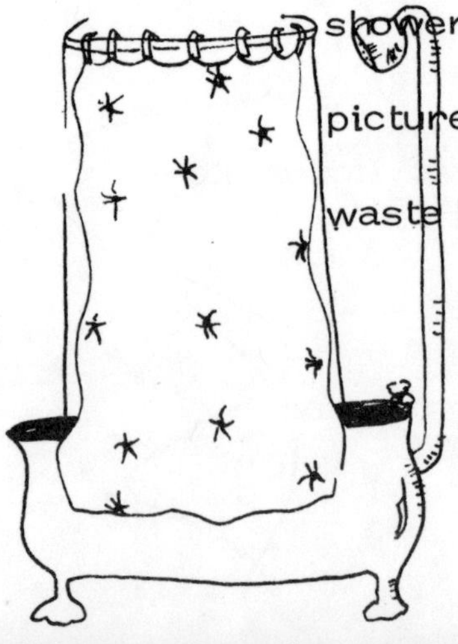

old textbooks and workbooks
..to cut apart

kites

gift wrap

clothespins

flower pots

cake and candy tins

small rocks

clothes hangers

soda pop cartons

pictures

record and book mailers

purses

yarn

small rugs

shower curtains

picture frames

waste baskets

and IDEAS..kept in
a file, notebook,
scrapbook, on tape,
or film.

shells

orange crates

magazines

travel brochures

pegboard

carpet scraps

hat boxes

small rugs

plastic tablecloths

old umbrellas

ice cream containers

plastic forks, spoons, and
knifes

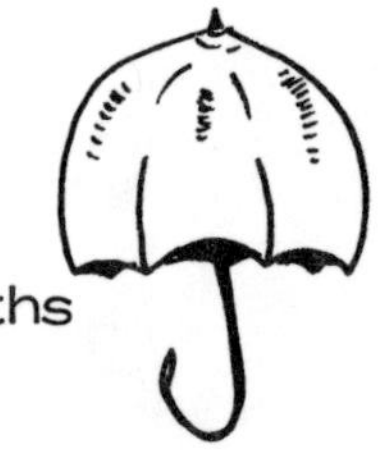

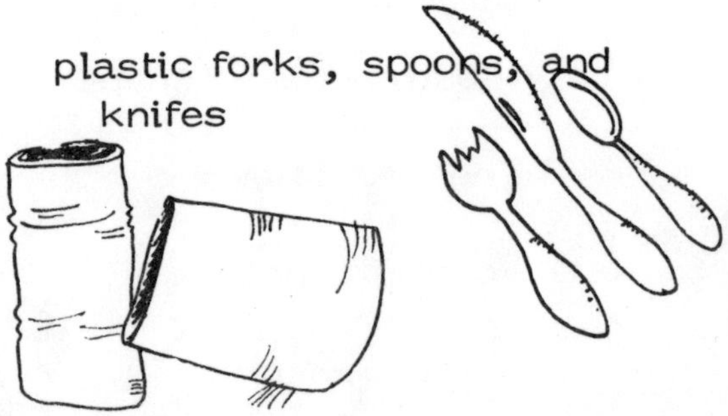

160

SELECTED TEACHER REFERENCES
An Annotated Listing of Kids' Stuff Learning Center Resources

Nooks, Crannies and Corners
by Imogene Forte and Joy MacKenzie

A simple question-answer format presenting solutions to common problems related to individualized teaching and to the learning center approach. Suggestions for creating the environment and making the transition from traditional to individualized instruction. Student assessment, record keeping, use of teacher made and commercial materials and classroom management made this book a practical teachers' guide.

Center Stuff for Nooks, Crannies and Corners
by Imogene Forte, Mary Ann Pangle and Robbie Tupa

More than fifty actual learning centers in math, science, social studies, and language arts to be used in either open space or traditional classrooms. Each model center contains performance objectives, an accounting of the materials needed and procedures for implementation, and coded student activity sheets on four levels of difficulty to be clipped out and reproduced for center use.

More Center Stuff for Nooks, Crannies and Corners
by Imogene Forte and Mary Ann Pangle

Identical in format to Center Stuff. Features fifty-six additional centers with all new subjects and content.

Cornering Creative Writing
by Imogene Forte, Mary Ann Pangle and Robbie Tupa

Fifty-two illustrated creative writing centers planned to be used as free choice interest centers to allow student flexibility, games to help students master basic skills and the mechanics of writing, and eighteen pages of special "Teacher Tactics" to help teachers create an environment to challenge children to write honestly, sensitively, and beautifully.

Pumpkins, Pinwheels and Peppermint Packages, Teacher Edition
  by Imogene Forte, Mary Ann Pangle and Robbie Tupa

Thirty-eight centers and more than three hundred fifty activities designed to help children develop appreciation for American traditions, events, and holidays. Each learning center is completely illustrated and contains activities in communications, creative arts, environmental studies, and quantitative studies; a puzzle or game; and a smorgasbord of "just for fun" ideas.

Pumpkins, Pinwheels and Peppermint Packages, Student Edition
  by Imogene Forte, Mary Ann Pangle and Robbie Tupa

Two hundred thirty-eight ready-to-reproduce pupil pages designed to accompany the activities presented in the hardback teacher edition. (This book serves as companion to but may be used independently of the teacher edition.)

Special Kids' Stuff
  by Cherrie Farnette, Imogene Forte and Barbara Loss

A simple format featuring easy-to-follow directions and limited vocabulary, and introduces high interest activity centers presented at three levels of difficulty. Study projects, student contracts, learning centers, activity cards, and illustrated reproducable work sheets provide humor and creative opportunity for skill development on an individual or group basis.

For additional activities, techniques, and procedures to use in a learning center setting see:

> Kids' Stuff, Reading and Writing Readiness
> Kids' Stuff, Reading and Language Experiences, Primary
> Kids' Stuff, Reading and Language Experiences, Intermediate-Jr. High
> Kids' Stuff, Math
> Kids' Stuff, Social Studies
> Games Without Losers
> Spelling Magic

Notes

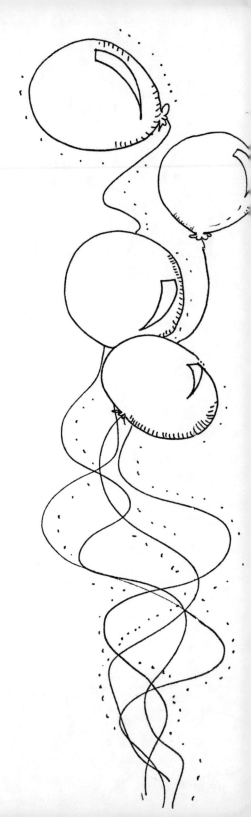